Cooking from Memory

Cooking from Memory

A Journey through Jewish Food

Hardie Grant Books

HAYLEY SMORGON * GAYE WEEDEN * NATALIE KING

PHOTOGRAPHY BY MARK ROPER

Published in 2006
by Hardie Grant Books
85 High Street
Prahran, Victoria
3181, Australia
www.hardiegrant.com.au

National Library of Australia Cataloguing-in-Publication Data:

Smorgon, Hayley.
Cooking from memory : a journey through
Jewish food.
Includes index.
ISBN 1 74066 286 5.
1. Cookery, Jewish. I. Weeden, Gaye.
II. King, Natalie, 1966– . III. Roper, Mark
(Mark Earl). IV. Title.

641.5676

Jacket and text design by Trisha Garner
Photography by Mark Roper
Typeset by Pauline Haas, bluerinse setting
Printed and bound in China by SNP Leefung

*Wherever possible, all dates and historical
events have been checked and authenticated.
This is not a historical record; rather, it's a
series of personal stories told by Jewish migrants.
A shopping guide for specialty ingredients is
available at www.hardiegrant.com.au*

10 9 8 7 6 5 4 3 2 1

Contents

INTRODUCTION   vi

EASTERN EUROPE   1
    GEORGIA   2
    POLAND   9
    RUSSIA   17

WESTERN EUROPE   25
    FRANCE   26
    HUNGARY   33
    ITALY   40
    SCOTLAND   49

MIDDLE EAST   57
    IRAQ   58
    ISRAEL   65
    LEBANON   78

ASIA   85
    INDIA   86
    INDONESIA   95
    JAPAN   103
    UZBEKISTAN   110
    VIETNAM   119

AFRICA   127
    LIBYA   128
    MOROCCO   136
    SOUTH AFRICA   143
    ZIMBABWE   152

THE AMERICAS   159
    ARGENTINA   160
    UNITED STATES OF AMERICA   172

GLOSSARY   179

INDEX   181

ACKNOWLEDGEMENTS   185

Introduction

'Every cuisine tells a story. Jewish food tells the story of an uprooted, migrating people and their vanished worlds.' Claudia Roden

Records show that at least seven Jews arrived in Botany Bay with the First Fleet in 1788. Among them was Esther Abrahams, who had been tried at the Old Bailey for stealing lace valued at fifty shillings. Arrested when she was in her teens and pregnant, Esther gave birth to a daughter in Newgate prison. She was sentenced to seven years and left England soon afterwards. While on the journey to Australia with her daughter, she formed a liaison with Lieutenant George Johnston, then aged twenty-three. Johnston would become a leading player in the events of the colony, suppressing revolts and rebellions, and eventually declaring himself Lieutenant Governor. Esther Abrahams would become the First Lady of New South Wales.

The story of Esther's journey to Australia is a tale of exile, migration and resettlement. And it is not unfamiliar: there are numerous tales of separation and loss, accounts of miracles and tragedy, from those who have formed the Jewish Diaspora in Australia. This book contains twenty-one such stories, from as many countries, giving a fascinating account of Jewish migration to Australia. But the common thread in this collection is the telling of how food and flavours fill the Jewish home with love, how food has always been a source of sustenance, joy and togetherness. Today, the act of cooking is not just a physical process; it represents the passion that bonds each cook to their homeland and ancestry. Here is an indelible link to the past and the future: a culinary voyage.

Jewish festivals are celebrated with feasts and customs. The Sabbath – the Jewish day of rest and spiritual rejuvenation – begins on Friday at sunset, ushered into the home with the lighting of candles and the blessing of wine and bread. A festive meal follows. In Australia, we are fortunate to have multicultural influences on our Jewish cuisine as people from all corners of the globe have settled here, bringing their Jewish culinary skills and influences that range from the impeccable presentation of Japanese cuisine to the abundance of mezze-style Iraqi food.

Many of the cooks featured in this book prepare their dishes from memory, so participating in this project gave them a unique opportunity to transcribe their time-honoured heritage while telling personal tales of displacement and reunion, separation and celebration. Each cook prepared signature dishes and welcomed us into their home to share precious food as well as memories, laughter, tears and captivating stories. In doing so, every one of them has opened their hearts and doors for a wider audience of food lovers, generously sharing their traditions. Balancing flavour, texture, colour and ingredients, each cook draws on culinary traditions that have evolved over centuries, passed down through families and adapted to contemporary Australian life.

Some dishes are simple, made from the freshest ingredients, while others are complex and elaborate. There is the spicy fragrance of Indian curry, the sumptuousness of Sephardi couscous and the now legendary chicken soup and gefilte fish from Ashkenazi cooking. We have also included the unique cuisines of ethnic groups such as Bukhara, with its cholent inventively cooked in a bag, and the organic, healthy food of Georgia. As you explore the following pages, we hope you will savour this delectable and inspiring journey.

Natalie King, Hayley Smorgon and Gaye Weeden

Eastern Europe
Georgia, Poland, Russia

A HEARTY CUISINE, EASTERN EUROPEAN COOKING CONTAINS MANY VEGETABLES AND FRUITS, OFTEN PRESERVED, PICKLED AND STORED IN CELLARS OVER THE FREEZING WINTER MONTHS. RELYING ON LOCAL PRODUCE, THIS PEASANT-STYLE COOKING COMPRISES STEWS, SOUPS AND DUMPLINGS THAT WARM AND NOURISH THE SOUL. POTATOES ARE A MAINSTAY IN THE REGION, WHICH IS PRIMARILY DEVOTED TO FARMING AND AGRICULTURE. THE UNIQUE TRADITIONS AND CUSTOMS OF THE ASHKENAZI JEWS OF EASTERN EUROPE EVOLVED OVER CENTURIES. IN THE PAST, ASHKENAZIM TENDED TO LIVE IN GHETTOS (OR SHTETLACH) SEGREGATED FROM THE NON-JEWISH POPULATION. THEY SPOKE YIDDISH, A COMBINATION OF GERMAN AND HEBREW WRITTEN IN HEBREW SCRIPT, AND WERE SUSTAINED BY POTS OF CHICKEN SOUP. ASHKENAZI FOOD IS USUALLY COOKED IN CHICKEN OR GOOSE FAT, ENRICHED WITH GOLDEN ONIONS.

Luba Kojia GEORGIA

Wherever I lived, I cooked Georgian food.
In Vienna, all my friends would bring over different dishes
from their respective cuisines – Bukharan, Russian and
Ukrainian – for our gatherings. Georgian food is so
special and tasty, with lots of flavours and spices.
Everyone who tries Georgian cuisine loves it.

BORN after the war in 1946, Luba and her twin brother Eugene lived in an apartment in central Kiev with their parents and older brother Benny, from a first marriage. Their mother, Esther, was a surgical nurse, while their father, Arkady, was a mechanic who made and repaired sewing machines for his successful business. As a soldier during the war, Arkady sustained a terrible injury that put him on a priority list for a better home.

When Luba was twelve, the family moved to a beautiful, spacious apartment. Initially the basement was used for residential purposes but eventually it became a cellar to store produce for the freezing winter months. In advance, they prepared pickled tomatoes, cucumbers and mushrooms as well as fruit compote stored in glass jars. They made chocolate spread, strawberry jam and pickled apples in airtight containers. Fresh produce was purchased from a large market about three kilometres from their home. Farmers from the countryside brought their produce to this market and Luba remembers carrying home bundles of food.

Luba had many Jewish friends in Kiev, with its thriving Jewish community of 250,000. There was only one synagogue, which was virtually impossible to attend because of the large crowds that flocked there on holy days. There were no Jewish schools, so Luba went to the local public school along with her siblings. After school she took gymnastics and dance classes, and learned English. At college, Luba studied geophysical economics and took a job with a mining company after graduation. She frequently travelled to Moscow and Leningrad for the official authority to sell valuable mining machines.

On Passover, Luba's mother and grandmother Tatiana prepared chicken soup, gefilte fish and charoset – a symbolic dish that is a mixture of grated apples, crushed nuts and wine. Matzo was difficult to obtain as it was forbidden by the government, so they went to a secret manufacturer for the unleavened bread for seder night. Luba's mother, a talented cook, prepared Jewish food such as Ukrainian borscht and dumplings. Luba used to watch her cook for the family. Her grandmother always prepared the Sabbath meal at their house.

In 1973, Luba migrated to Israel and settled in Rishon L'tzion, known as the first Israeli city, a short distance from Tel Aviv. Although the Russian Government was strict in granting exit visas, Luba arrived with her family to follow Benny, who had already migrated. She went on an ulpan to learn Hebrew and started working in the central office of the Department of Defence. Soon afterwards,

she met, and married, a Georgian named Michael, who was an economist for the taxation office. Two months after her arrival, the Yom Kippur War broke out.

Luba watched and helped her mother-in-law cook and soon started preparing and transcribing her unique recipes. In no time, she was besotted with Georgian cuisine. 'All my cooking is inspired by my mother-in-law, Zina. She was an excellent cook. Every Saturday she made ten different dishes. She spent all day in the kitchen, even after the guests arrived.'

Georgians enjoy longevity due to their diet of organic food and fresh produce. Clean mountain air and a temperate climate ensure that fruit, vegetables and lamb are plentiful. Georgian Jews don't eat gefilte fish. Instead, the mainstay of any Georgian table is lobio, a dish of red or green kidney beans, which grow wild, flavoured with chilli and coriander.

Many fresh herbs are used in Georgian cooking, which tends to be spicy, and a variety of salads are served with every meal. Luba enjoys preparing chanahi – a lamb and vegetable stew with eggplant, red and green capsicum, coriander, dill, garlic and onions. Another favourite among Georgian Jews is kharcho – a thick, hearty soup with lamb, rice, onions, garlic, celery, turmeric and chilli. Presentation is crucial, with dishes served on ornate platters ensuring that the table is laden with food – 'the table must be full'. Pomegranates are a common ingredient – sometimes their tiny, jewel-like beads are transformed into a thick molasses.

After seven years in Israel, the family decided they wanted to travel. Luba and Michael departed for England in 1979 with their two daughters, Regina and Lina. After a visit to Michael's childhood friend from Georgia, Ivango, who was living in London, Michael started working as a diamond setter. The family relocated to Vienna for Michael's work, but as they only had a tourist visa, it was extremely difficult to stay. Many of their friends were applying for migration permits to Australia but only Luba and Michael were granted permission, probably because of their professional qualifications. Previously, they had been refused permits to go to the United States, where Luba's brother Eugene was living.

In 1981, the family arrived in Melbourne, where they shared an apartment with three Russian couples. Luba immediately began working for the government census while Michael found work as a diamond setter. She started to entertain guests in her home. Now, Luba's home is filled with family heirlooms, cabinets resplendent with ornate china, faceted glass cups in gold holders, and cobalt blue and gold tea sets that have travelled from Moscow to Melbourne. Speaking Russian with her children and grandchildren, she also understands the Georgian language. She is proudly carrying on her precious tradition: 'Now I cook from memory. I know how the taste should be.'

Georgian Lamb Soup

Kharcho

3 litres (5 pints) water

500 g (1 lb) lamb shanks or
veal osso bucco

2 onions, finely chopped

3–4 cloves garlic, minced

1 teaspoon ground turmeric

$\frac{1}{4}$ teaspoon dried chilli

1 stalk celery, chopped

1 x 440 g can tomatoes, finely chopped

3 tablespoons tomato paste

2 tablespoons vegetable stock powder

$\frac{3}{4}$ cup long-grain rice

salt

ground black pepper

$\frac{1}{2}$ bunch coriander, finely chopped

This is a hearty ethnic Georgian soup.

Boil water in a large saucepan. Add the lamb shanks, onions, garlic, spices, celery, tomatoes, tomato paste and stock powder. Cook for 1 hour on medium heat, until meat is soft. Skim any froth from the surface. Add the rice, and salt and pepper to taste. Cook for a further 20 minutes. Add coriander to the soup 5 minutes before serving.

Serves 12

Beetroot Salad

6 beetroot

100 g (3$\frac{1}{2}$ oz) ground almonds

100 g (3$\frac{1}{2}$ oz) ground hazelnuts

3 cloves garlic, minced

2 teaspoons organic apple cider vinegar

handful of coriander and dill,
finely chopped

salt

ground black pepper

Wash the beetroot and simmer whole in salted water on a low heat for 2–3 hours. Cool, peel and finely dice the beetroot. Mix the nuts with garlic, vinegar, coriander and dill, then combine with the beetroot. Add salt and pepper to taste, and serve at room temperature.

Serves 4

Bean Salad

Red Lobio Salad

The mainstay of any Georgian table, lobio is made from red or green kidney beans that grow wild, flavoured with chilli and coriander.

4 x 440 g cans 3-bean mix

4 spring onions, finely chopped

1 teaspoon salt

¼ teaspoon ground black pepper

½ bunch coriander, finely chopped

¼ fresh red chilli, finely chopped

Mix all ingredients together and serve.

Serves 6–8

Green Bean Dish

Green Lobio

1 kg (2 lb) green beans

2 onions, finely chopped

2 teaspoons vegetable stock powder

1 teaspoon salt

2 eggs

salt

ground black pepper

½ bunch coriander, finely chopped

String the beans and chop into small pieces, about 3 cm (1½ in) in length. Place them with the onions and stock powder in a saucepan, cover with water and add salt. Cook uncovered on a high heat, until the water has been absorbed. Beat the eggs and season with salt and pepper. Add to the beans and mix thoroughly while hot. Garnish with coriander. Serve hot.

Serves 4–6

Eastern Europe, Georgia

Opposite Chanahi

Chicken in a Mixed Nut Sauce

Satsivi

This dish is usually served for the Sabbath lunch as it can be eaten hot or at room temperature.

1 cooled chicken from Chicken Soup (page 12)

1 cup mixed ground hazelnuts, almonds and walnuts

3 cloves garlic, minced

¼ bunch coriander, finely chopped

¼ fresh chilli, finely chopped

2 cups Chicken Soup (page 12)

Chop the chicken into 10 pieces and place on a platter. In a bowl combine the mixed nuts, garlic, coriander and chilli with the chicken soup, then pour over the chicken pieces. Serve cold or hot.

Serves 4–6

Lamb Stew

Chanahi

Luba particularly enjoys preparing chanahi – a hearty lamb and vegetable stew.

1.5 kg (3 lb) lamb forequarter chops

3 eggplants, cut into long, fine strips

salt

10 potatoes, peeled and quartered

4 tomatoes, chopped

2 large onions, roughly chopped

1 green capsicum, cut into long, fine strips

1 red capsicum, cut into long, fine strips

4 cloves garlic, roughly chopped

½ bunch coriander, roughly chopped

¼ bunch dill, roughly chopped

3 tablespoons tomato paste

3 cups water

¼ fresh chilli, finely chopped

1 teaspoon salt

½ teaspoon ground black pepper

Preheat the oven to 200°C (400°F).

Place the lamb chops on a tray and roast for 20–25 minutes, until brown. Then transfer them to a casserole dish.

Salt the eggplant and allow it to sweat for half an hour, then rinse it and pat dry with paper towels. Cover the lamb with layers of potato, tomato, onion, capsicum and eggplant, then sprinkle garlic, coriander and dill over the top. Mix the tomato paste with the water, chilli, salt and pepper and pour over the casserole. Cover and bake at 200°C (400°F) for 50 minutes. Serve hot.

Serves 6–8

Shirley Hirsh POLAND

My mother-in-law, Gitl Hirsh, is my main inspiration.
I used to watch her cook, especially strudel. All her
children can prepare gefilte fish. She even made
her own lokshen. I have adapted many dishes
as I prefer healthy, simple cooking.

BORN in 1926 in the army city of Brest-Litowk, Szejna (later Shirley) spent her early childhood on the border of Poland and Russia. Her mother, Zlata, worked in the family's large dairy shop at the front of their house, where they produced homemade butter and cheese. With two sons and two daughters to raise, as well as a business, Zlata had scant time to cook for her family. Shirley's father, Don, had been in the Russian army and was a self-taught linguist who studied many languages, including Hebrew, Russian and Polish.

In 1935, the family lived through a Polish pogrom that violently ransacked the homes of Jews in their neighbourhood. The pogrom started in their street in a butcher's shop owned by a Jewish father and his son. Their meat required stamping for consumption but sometimes the Polish inspector confiscated it. The son eventually killed the inspector and while he was hiding in a neighbouring cellar the pogrom started. Shirley's family was hiding in an adjoining house owned by a high-ranking Polish army official who had taken them in to save their lives. After the pogrom, Zlata found that a large jar of schmaltz (chicken fat) that she'd had had been spitefully ruined with milk in order to make it non-kosher and therefore unusable.

During this period, there was extensive and disturbing anti-Semitism in Poland. Shirley recalls a neighbourhood friend taking her to meet some other children who later beat Shirley up. Her father used to go out to buy the American newspaper but he would hurry home so he didn't get knifed. People would stand outside their shop and tell customers, 'Don't shop in a Jewish store!' Shirley's father didn't want his children to suffer the way he had during World War I, when he was made to walk barefoot in the snow. With anti-Semitism threatening, the family decided to escape their unsettling environment.

They were unable to migrate to Palestine because they didn't make the quota. Shirley's father foresaw the war and decided to apply for migration permits to Australia. As farmers, they were granted preferential permits due to their agricultural knowledge, and within six weeks their papers were issued. Shirley migrated to Australia in 1938 at the age of twelve. Young Szejna's new Australian friends told her to call herself 'Shirley' because Shirley Temple was a popular actress and 'Szejna' was difficult to pronounce.

Initially, Shirley and her family lived for one year in Melbourne, but then relocated to the farming township of Shepparton, where the boys went to school on horses. Shirley's mother opened a shop,

but as she was orthodox, she couldn't open it for Saturday trading. They decided to live on a farm of twenty acres (eight hectares), which they were able to purchase with the help of Mr Faiglin, a wealthy man associated with Jewish Welfare who owned timber forests. They grew tomatoes, planted fruit trees and set up a dairy. Shirley recalls the struggle of these early years when they were not paid well for their produce. She quickly learned English but forgot her Polish, Russian and Hebrew, although she continued to speak Yiddish at home.

In 1944, six years after they arrived, her mother passed away. By this time, the family had already left Shepparton and owned a thriving grocery shop in Lygon Street, Carlton in inner-city Melbourne. When her father also died, Shirley was forced to leave school at fifteen in order to run the grocery store with her sister, Hanna, and younger brother, Joe, taking on the responsibility of their parents. The store was successful, enabling the children to buy property. Her other brother, Shalom, studied law and returned to Poland after the war to follow his communist ideals.

The first thing Shirley ever baked was a lemnos cake with three vivid colour elements – butter, chocolate and red colouring. Experimenting with these different colours, Shirley made a marble pattern. On another occasion, though, she bought half a pound of brisket, which she soaked and salted for cooking, even though it was already cooked!

Friends introduced Shirley to Jack Hirsh, who in 1926 had arrived in Australia from Lodz, Poland, at the age of two. He ran his own business, M Hirsh & Sons, manufacturing women's clothing. The couple were married in 1949 and their first child, Don, was born a year later, followed by Lynn, Mark and Gaye. Shirley worked intermittently in Jack's factory and eventually opened her own women's fashion boutique in the mid-1970s. Although she worked full-time, she prepared the Sabbath meal until midnight every Thursday.

Shirley's mother-in-law, Gitl, prepared Friday-night feasts, favouring gefilte fish, homemade lokshen and her famous apple strudel with three layers of butter pastry laid into a square tin with apple and cinnamon. 'She had the touch to make it just right,' Shirley remembers. 'All her children can make apple strudel.' Shirley makes her own version in the form of strudel biscuits, adapted to incorporate dried apricots, chocolate and jam as well as orange peel or cumquats.

Shirley enjoys adapting her own family's dishes and she still relishes making her mother's recipe for white cheese. For everyday eating, she prefers simple cooking such as grilled Atlantic salmon. But for the Sabbath, dishes are prepared in advance and include stewed fruit such as cherries and plums. A healthy cook with flair, Shirley enhances her food in simple ways: she rarely uses salt, preferring tamari instead, and buys organic produce. She makes apricot jam and still cooks inventive food for her large extended family and grandchildren. Her recipes are transcribed into a small book but she mainly cooks from memory: 'I enjoy cooking for my grandchildren. If they eat it, I enjoy it. Now, I share cooking with my daughters and daughter-in-law for the many guests on Friday night.'

Shirley Hirsh

Chicken Soup

Traditionally served on the Sabbath, chicken soup is often referred to as Jewish penicillin due to its medicinal qualities.

1 kg (2 lb) chicken thighs
4 chicken carcasses (frames)
2 onions
3 carrots, chopped
1 parsnip, chopped
3 stalks celery, chopped
6 litres (10 pints) water
3 chicken stock cubes

Rinse the chicken thighs and carcasses and place them in a large pot. Cover them with water and bring to the boil, skimming off any froth that comes to the surface. Add the remaining ingredients and simmer on a low heat for 2 hours, partially covered. (Boiling the soup rapidly will cause it to become cloudy.)

Set the soup aside to cool, then strain into another saucepan, discarding the vegetables and setting aside the chicken for other use, for example, to make Piroshkis. Refrigerate the soup overnight. Remove the layer of fat on the surface, reheat and serve, or freeze for later use.

Serves 12

Feather-light Matzo Balls
Kneidlach

These delicious soup dumplings are served on Passover as they don't contain bread.

2 eggs
80 ml (3 fl oz) light olive oil
1 cup coarse matzo meal
¼ to ½ cup water
pinch of salt
¼ teaspoon ground ginger or cinnamon (optional)

Mix the eggs, oil and matzo meal until well combined. Add water and salt, and stir to make a batter. Add the ginger, cover and refrigerate for at least 2 hours.

Wash your hands with cold water and, with moist hands, form balls the size of a walnut. Drop the balls into salted boiling water in a large saucepan and partially cover with lid. Boil for 30 minutes or until the balls float to the top and swell. To make them softer, cook longer. Drain and serve with clear Chicken Soup (above).

Makes 6–8

Opposite (front to back) Chicken Soup and Gefilte Fish

Jewish Spring Rolls

Piroshki

2 tablespoons olive oil

2 onions, finely chopped

3 carrots, grated

½ teaspoon dried oregano

½ teaspoon ground black pepper

½ roast chicken or leftover boiled chicken from Chicken Soup (page 12), shredded

200 g (7 oz) thin rice noodles

1 packet wonton wrappers

Heat 1 tablespoon of oil in a frying pan and sauté onions until brown. Add the carrots and stir until they soften. Sprinkle with oregano and pepper, stir the chicken through and set aside.

Break the noodles into small pieces, about 10 cm (4 in) in length, and submerge in a bowl of boiling water for 5 minutes. Rinse with cold water, strain, and refrigerate for easier handling.

Place each wonton wrapper in a diamond shape on a flat surface. Spoon a small amount of chicken mixture below the top corner. Fold the corner over the filling, roll once, fold in the sides and continue rolling.

Heat 1 tablespoon of olive oil in a deep frying pan. Shallow-fry piroshki until golden brown. Drain on paper towels. Serve or freeze when cool.

Makes 6

Fish Balls

Gefilte Fish

Traditionally eaten on the Sabbath and Jewish New Year, these cold fish balls vary according to region. The added sugar is a distinctive Polish variant. Gefilte fish is best served the day after cooking.

STOCK

2 litres (3½ pints) water

Murray perch bones

1 large carrot, thickly sliced

1 onion, thickly sliced

½ teaspoon salt

½ teaspoon ground white pepper

1 tablespoon sugar

FISH

1.5 kg (3 lb) Murray perch, minced

500 g (1 lb) flathead fillets, minced

250 g (9 oz) sea perch fillets, minced

2 onions, finely chopped

pinch of salt

ground white pepper to taste

1 tablespoon sugar

3 eggs, beaten

1 hard-boiled egg, mashed

50 g (2 oz) matzo meal

¼ cup soda water

Ask your fishmonger to skin, bone and mince the fish, retaining bones for stock.

To make the stock, pour water into a large saucepan and bring to the boil. Add remaining stock ingredients and boil for 30 minutes. (Do not overcook, as stock will become bitter.) Strain through a fine sieve, reserving the carrot for garnish.

To prepare the fish, mix the mince, onions, salt, pepper and sugar. Add beaten and hard-boiled eggs, matzo meal and soda water. Mix well with a metal spoon. Mixture should be firm. Refrigerate it for several hours, then, with moist hands, roll the mixture into oval balls. Bring the stock to the boil and add fish balls. Simmer gently for 1 hour, remove fish balls and refrigerate. Serve chilled, garnished with a slice of cooked carrot.

Makes 20

Roast Chicken

For greater succulence, balance the chicken on its side while roasting.

1.5 kg (3 lb) chicken
1 tablespoon honey
1 tablespoon tamari
¼ teaspoon freshly ground black pepper
4 cloves garlic, minced
juice of 2 oranges or lemons
2 cups hot water

Preheat the oven to 200°C (400°F).

Wash the chicken well in cold water. Pour boiling water over it quickly and then repeat with ice-cold water. Pat the chicken dry with paper towels inside and out, then drizzle honey and tamari over it. Add pepper, garlic and orange juice. Pour water along the bottom of a baking pan and roast the chicken for 90 minutes, rotating every half hour. If the water evaporates, add more. To make gravy, sieve pan juices and serve on the side.

Serves 5

Strudel Biscuits

Rugelach

Shirley is famous for her strudel biscuits and found it difficult to part with the recipe that was passed down from her mother-in-law, Gitl.

1 egg white

icing sugar for dusting

PASTRY

250 g (9 oz) unsalted butter, cubed

1¾ cups self-raising flour

1¾ cups plain flour

1 egg yolk

200 ml (7 fl oz) sour cream

flour for dusting bench top

FILLING

620 g (1¼ lb) apricot or plum jam

50 g (1½ oz) dark chocolate, melted

rind of 1 orange, grated

200 g (7 oz) dried apricots, currants, prunes or sultanas, chopped

To make the pastry, blend the butter and flour in a food processor until the mixture resembles fine breadcrumbs. Add egg yolk and sour cream and blend until the dough forms a ball. Wrap dough in plastic wrap and refrigerate for at least 2 hours.

To make the filling, combine jam, chocolate, orange rind and dried fruit.

Divide the dough into seven equal portions. Roll each portion on a cool, floured surface into a thin rectangle, about 15 cm x 30 cm (6 in x 12 in). Spread filling onto each and, starting at one end, roll up.

Preheat the oven to 200°C (400°F).

Line a baking tray with baking paper. Cut the pastry into 2 cm (¾ in) pieces and place pieces on the tray a few centimetres apart. Brush the pastry with egg white and bake for 25 minutes, until golden brown. Dust with icing sugar before serving.

Makes about 50

Eastern Europe, Poland

Susie Roitman RUSSIA

I love and enjoy cooking. It gives me pleasure when people find my cooking tasty. My grandchildren prefer Australian food but I love European food. I try to make the most of everything. If you want to do something, you can. I am very determined.

SUSIE grew up in Lvov, where she was born in 1948. Now part of the Ukraine, Lvov was Russian with a Polish influence when Susie was a child. This beautiful city came to be known as 'little Vienna' because so many of its buildings resemble lavish Viennese architecture. Susie lived in the old part of the city with her younger brother, Sam, their father, Benjamin, an accountant, and their mother, Anna, a paediatric cardiologist.

Susie recalls many tourists visiting her famous neighbourhood, where she lived with her grandparents and aunt. Their home was a large flat with high, ornate ceilings, exquisite doors and gleaming parquetry. Susie grew up in a cultured environment, regularly attending the theatre and ballet while her family strongly emphasised the importance of education. Choir and dance classes were compulsory at school. The family spoke Yiddish, Polish and Russian at home.

Despite her father's orthodoxy, Susie attended a secular school, housed in an old building from 1807, where she was a class convenor. Many of her teachers were Jewish. Growing up in a communist environment, she was taught their principles as a young girl. In the early 1960s, the synagogue was closed and Jews had to pray in private homes. As a result, on Yom Kippur Susie's mother used to pray at a nearby home that was converted to a house of worship.

Susie's mother cooked Russian food and she especially adored baking. She often made Napoleon – puff pastry with custard, similar to a vanilla slice – and a substantial lunch was always served in the dining room. She taught her daughter to make pirochki and vareniki – sweet or savoury boiled dumplings served with sour cream or butter. On Passover, borscht was garnished with broken matzo, either hot or cold.

Russian food is a hearty cuisine, partly because of the extreme climate. Susie and her mother would go to the market to purchase seasonal produce. In spring, they selected radishes, spring onions and cucumbers to make salads, while autumn was a frenetic time for the family as they stocked up on hundred-kilogram bags of potatoes, apples and onions to be stored in a cellar under the house. Pickled cucumbers and sour cabbage were kept in wooden barrels as supplies for the family over the freezing winter. Fruits and vegetables were preserved in sterilised glass jars, as were cherry and apricot jams. Like a factory, this stockpiling involved many family members gathering together to help. Any fruits that could not be obtained fresh for preserving, such as prunes or apricots, would be bought dried, then later stewed as a compote with cinnamon quills.

At the age of twelve, when Susie was in Year 5, she met her future husband, Igor. They married in 1968, when Susie was twenty, and their daughter was born the following year. Having promised her father that she would complete her higher education, Susie finished university during this intense time. From the moment she married, she started cooking just like her mother, often phoning her to ask for advice. She believes cooking 'comes naturally, by observation'.

When their daughter, Alla, was two and a half, the couple decided to leave Russia due to the oppressive conditions of the Soviet regime. In 1972, the family went to Israel via Vienna where they were met by the Jewish migration and refugee resettlement agency, the Hebrew Immigrant Aid Society, who provided an allowance for rent and food while they were in transit. The family settled in Holon, nine kilometres from Tel Aviv. Susie learned Hebrew swiftly and worked as an economic accountant.

Eleven months later, the Yom Kippur War began and Igor was sent to the Golan Heights. During this period, he came home for brief visits of twenty-four hours but was forbidden to reveal his whereabouts. After the war, Igor was eager to leave Israel, so the family went to Rome with Israeli passports, awaiting visas for the United States. Both the US and Canada refused visas but Australia granted them to ten families and, fortunately, Susie's was third on the list.

Far from Europe, they had never dreamed of coming to Australia, where they arrived in 1977 with three suitcases. Susie vividly recalls the strange drive from the airport. Ultimately, they realised they had made the best choice: 'It's a lucky and safe country for children and grandchildren.' They appreciate the education and culture in Australia, where Susie attends the theatre and has learned to make tapestries and jewellery, while Igor has been able to pursue his love of musicals. Alla inherited her parents' musicality and took lessons from a young age, practising on a piano that Susie and Igor managed to purchase by working hard in their new country.

Susie now dines frequently in Russian Jewish restaurants in her neighbourhood and sources her favourite ingredients in a nearby Jewish shopping centre. Every two years, Susie's mother visits from Israel and makes a vast supply of pirochki and cabbage rolls to last for one year! Now, Alla enjoys baking with her grandmother's treasured recipes.

Susie Roitman

Beetroot Soup

Borscht

This beetroot soup has a beautiful pink colour. On Passover it is served, either hot or cold,
with broken matzo. It can also be made without meat.

1 kg (2 lb) beef top rib

2 beef marrow bones

3 litres (5 pints) water

2 beetroot, peeled

3 carrots, peeled

1 stalk celery

1 brown onion

½ head green cabbage, shredded

3 potatoes, cubed

juice of 1 lemon

½ teaspoon brown sugar

salt

ground black pepper

1 clove garlic, minced

2 tablespoons tomato paste or
1 x 440 ml can tomato soup

½ bunch parsley or dill, chopped

Bring the meat, bones and water to the boil in a large pot. Skim off any froth that comes to the surface. Add whole beetroot, carrots, celery and onion to the saucepan, cover and reduce the heat to low. Simmer for 1–1½ hours, until the meat is cooked.

Strain the stock and separate the meat from the bones. Set aside the meat.

When cool, grate the beetroot and carrots and finely chop the onion. Return them to the stock liquid and add the cabbage, potatoes and lemon juice to the saucepan. Cook for 10–15 minutes on a medium heat. Add the sugar, salt, pepper, garlic, tomato paste, parsley and reserved meat. Bring to the boil and serve hot, or refrigerate and serve cold.

Serves 10–12

Russian Potato Salad

6 potatoes, unpeeled

6 eggs

3 carrots

1 x 680 g jar dill pickled cucumbers

1 x 440 g can green peas

100 g (3½ oz) mayonnaise

salt

ground black pepper

Boil whole potatoes, eggs and carrots in water until firm, about 20 minutes. Chop the cucumbers. Drain, cool and peel the potatoes, carrots and eggs, and cut into small cubes. Place them in a large bowl with the cucumbers and peas. Dress with mayonnaise and season to taste.

Serves 10–12

Opposite Borscht

Savoury Dumplings

Pirochki

Susie's mother taught her to make pirochki – savoury dumplings served with sour cream or butter.
Pirochki may be frozen but should not be defrosted before baking.

3 onions, finely chopped

1 kg (2 lb) mushrooms, finely chopped

3 tablespoons olive oil

2 kg (4 lb) minced beef or chicken, boiled

salt

ground black pepper

1.5 kg (3 lb) prepared puff pastry

1 egg, beaten

Preheat the oven to 200°C (400°F).

Sauté the onions and mushrooms in olive oil in a deep frying pan until they soften and the onion is slightly browned. Add the meat and mix through. Season to taste and set aside.

Lightly grease a large baking tray. Roll out the pastry on a floured surface. With a large-rimmed glass, cut out rounds of about 8 cm (3 in) in diameter. Alternatively, use a knife to cut squares. Put a heaped teaspoon of the filling in the centre of each round or square and fold over to form a semicircle or triangle. Press the edges with a fork to seal. Place dumplings on the baking tray and brush them with egg.

Lower the oven temperature to 180°C (350°F) and bake for 20–25 minutes, until golden brown.

Makes about 50

Cabbage Rolls

1 onion, chopped

2 tablespoons olive oil

1 carrot, finely chopped

750 g (1½ lb) minced chicken

½ cup basmati rice, washed

1 large head green cabbage

1 x 440 ml can tomato soup

280 g tomato paste

salt

ground black pepper

1 teaspoon brown sugar

In a deep saucepan sauté the onion in olive oil until it softens. Add the carrot and sauté until softened. Add mince and stir continuously until meat is cooked through, breaking up any lumps with a fork. Gently add the rice and mix for a couple of minutes. Set aside.

Remove its core and submerge the cabbage in a large saucepan of boiling water for about 20–25 minutes, or until the cabbage leaves may be removed without tearing. Remove all the leaves, keeping them in the boiling water until they are soft enough to roll. Then rinse them under cold water, drain and pat dry with paper towels.

Trim the tough vein in the centre of each leaf. Put about 1 tablespoon of the meat mixture in the centre of each cabbage leaf. Roll up, tucking in the sides as you go. Arrange the cabbage rolls, seam side down, in a large saucepan.

Combine 1 can of tomato soup and 2 cans of water, tomato paste, salt, pepper and sugar in a bowl and pour over the cabbage rolls. Cover the saucepan and bring to the boil. Reduce the heat and simmer for about 2 hours or until cabbage is tender. Serve hot.

Makes 15–20

Susie Roitman

Rice with Lamb and Pineapple

Plof

*A Russian rice dish made with lamb, this has a hint of natural sweetness
from the pineapple juice and carrots.*

80 ml (3 fl oz) olive oil

4–5 onions, chopped

3 carrots, grated

1.5 kg (3 lb) trimmed lamb, cubed

300 g (11 oz) basmati or jasmine rice, washed

juice from 440 g can unsweetened pineapple

3–4 cloves garlic, minced

salt

ground black pepper

Heat the oil in a non-stick saucepan and sauté the onions and carrots until softened. Add the lamb and cook, covered, on a low heat until meat is cooked through, about 1–1½ hours.

Add the rice, pineapple juice, garlic, salt and pepper to the saucepan and cover with boiling water about a finger's width above the rice and meat mixture.

Cook uncovered until the water evaporates and the rice is al dente. Remove from heat, place a tea towel over the saucepan and cover with the lid. Leave to rest for 10–15 minutes. Serve hot.

Serves 8–10

Sweet Dumplings

Vareniki

*Vareniki can be made with a variety of fillings – either sweet or savoury.
This recipe is for sweet vareniki.*

salt

1 teaspoon olive oil

300 ml (11 fl oz) sour cream

DOUGH

2 cups plain flour

1 cup boiling water

½ teaspoon salt

FILLING

250 ml (9 fl oz) full-cream continental cream cheese

2 tablespoons caster sugar

½ teaspoon vanilla essence

Combine flour, water and salt in a bowl to form a dough.

To make the filling, combine the cheese, sugar and vanilla essence in a bowl and set aside.

Divide the dough into 4–5 portions. On a lightly floured surface roll out each portion so that it is about 1 cm (½ in) thick. Cut the dough into rounds using a standard glass, and put a heaped teaspoon of the filling in the centre of each round. Fold in half to form a semicircle, pressing the air out with your fingers. Pinch the edges of the dough to seal.

Drop dumplings in several batches into a large saucepan of salted boiling water with a teaspoon of olive oil. Reduce the heat. Do not stir. When the vareniki rise to the surface, remove them from the water with a slotted spoon and drain in a colander. Serve hot with a dollop of sour cream.

Makes 30

Western Europe
France, Hungary, Italy, Scotland

RICH IN TRADITION AND DIVERSITY, WESTERN EUROPEAN CUISINE REFLECTS THE MULTI-ETHNICITY OF THE JEWISH PEOPLE AND THE MANY PLACES WHERE THEY HAVE SETTLED. UNIQUE DISHES HAVE EVOLVED WITH LOCAL INFLUENCES — SUCH AS THE CREAMY SAUCES OF FRENCH COOKING, THE PIQUANT FLAVOUR OF HUNGARIAN PAPRIKA AND THE WHOLESOMENESS OF SCOTTISH DISHES. GRAINS AND BEANS ARE EATEN IN ABUNDANCE: HEALTHY, HEARTY AND FILLING. SOME SAY THE CASSOULET OF SOUTH-WEST FRANCE WAS ORIGINALLY CHOLENT, THE STEW BAKED IN A SLOW OVEN AND SERVED WARM ON THE SABBATH. IT IS ALSO THOUGHT THAT CHOCOLATE CAME TO FRANCE WITH THE SEPHARDI JEWS EXPELLED FROM SPAIN.

Suzanne Ress FRANCE

Western Europe

I love the creativity of cooking. I call it 'baking with passion.' My husband doesn't eat desserts in restaurants because he gets better at home. I have accumulated over two hundred recipes. I want to preserve them for my granddaughter.

A SELF-TAUGHT cook, Suzanne spent her early childhood in an apartment in the Marais district of Paris. The oldest of five sisters, Suzanne also has an older brother, George. Both her parents were from Warsaw but went to Brussels, then to Paris, where they established a millinery. Suzanne's mother, Marie, was a typical Jewish mother, busily looking after her large family. An excellent cook, she fused traditional Jewish dishes with French cuisine, preparing onion soup, escalope Milanese and grilled meat. On the Sabbath, she cooked chicken soup, roast or Provençale chicken and tarte aux pommes. Marie baked her own challah and kugelhopf, and incorporated the popular French ingredients tarragon and watercress into her French dishes. Not surprisingly, many of the children's friends came to visit, as the household was bustling like a restaurant.

In 1942, when Suzanne was eight, the Germans occupied Paris. Her father went into hiding and Marie didn't believe that the French police would arrest a woman with five children. When the police eventually arrived, Marie offered them money and jewellery in a futile attempt to save her children. The family were taken to an indoor velodrome stadium at Drancy just outside Paris. From there, Jews were sent to Auschwitz. In the stadium, names were being called out in alphabetical order for deportation, so Suzanne's mother pretended that she was pregnant and haemorrhaging. Frantically trying to save the lives of her young family, she started screaming and was taken to the infirmary in an ambulance, with her frightened children nearby. Later, when the doctor appeared, she hit him so hard that he was unable to examine her but he signed the papers that she was pregnant.

Marie and her children went to hide in St Agil, a small village outside Paris. The mayor gave the family false papers, even though the Gestapo headquarters were only a few doors from the house. In 1944, a Gestapo captain became fond of Marie and wanted to make a rendezvous with her, so Marie arranged for a peasant to collect her children from the roadside and the family fled to another village. Suzanne recalls the surreal moment of liberation as she was walking with her family to the village, when German tanks departed and American troops tossed flowers and chocolate. A few months later, her father returned from hiding in Switzerland and the family started rebuilding their lives.

During the war, Suzanne's brother George was like a father in the way he protected his younger sisters. In 1953, he migrated to Australia to see their cousin Maurice and to seek a better future for his sisters. Suzanne wept for months at the absence of her beloved brother. In 1955, George opened Mokaris, one of the first coffee shops in Melbourne, complete with an impressive Gaggia machine. In the meantime, Suzanne and her sister Rosette studied fashion design in Paris for two years. Since

they enjoyed going out dancing, the sisters would purchase patterns and fabric to fit each other with beautiful dresses – partly out of necessity because the family, having lost everything during the war, couldn't afford to buy clothes for the girls.

Believing in fate, Suzanne decided to follow her brother to Australia in 1955. Something urged her to leave her close-knit family and bravely embark on an Italian ship for the four-week journey to Melbourne. She arrived alone, in her early twenties. Soon after her arrival, Suzanne attended the wedding of Thelma and Lionel Meerkin at the local synagogue, where a young man, Leon Ress, was in the bridal party. Leon was transfixed by Suzanne. When he enquired as to her name, he realised the remarkable fact that it was already in his address book; his friend Maurice had passed on Suzanne's contact details just before Leon's recent journey to Paris, although Leon never contacted her. Leon had even travelled to Paris on the very ship on which Suzanne journeyed to Australia. Serendipity brought them together. They were engaged four months later and were married in the same synagogue.

The Ress family had been in the hotel industry for sixty years and at that time they owned the Ress Oriental Hotel in Collins Street. Suzanne lived with Leon on the first floor while her in-laws, Mick and Chifra Ress, occupied the third floor. No one lived in the city then, but vivacious Suzanne adjusted easily to this cosmopolitan lifestyle. Reminded of the Champs-Elysées, she suggested to her husband that they could put tables, chairs and umbrellas on the sidewalk. With an entrepreneurial streak, Leon approached the City of Melbourne and soon secured approval. The 'Paris end of Collins Street' was born. Living in the Ress Oriental Hotel for thirteen years, Suzanne gave birth to daughter Nicole and twin boys Philip and Michael. Sadly, Suzanne's mother passed away while she was pregnant with the twins.

There were three restaurants in the hotel – a Persian Room, a Harlequin Room and a steak house for businessmen – and many hotel guests were famous performers from abroad. Despite being surrounded by a life of excitement, Suzanne was keen to preserve family life, so she cooked meals at home and visited the nearby Fitzroy Gardens with her children. Even so, they had a hectic social life, especially with Leon being a councillor with the City of Melbourne. Avidly reading French magazines and books, Suzanne started baking for family and friends and her cooking maintained a strong French influence. In 1980, Leon purchased the Fawkner Club and the couple opened an elegant restaurant called Tiffany's on the Park. One night the pastry chef walked out after an argument with the head chef and, with two wall ovens at home, Suzanne was required to bake tarte aux fruits, chocolate mousse gâteau and chocolate roulade for the restaurant.

'People say I am a good baker but I've got plenty to learn,' she confesses. 'I feel like I can always improve myself.' Suzanne's photo album is bursting with images of her elaborate cakes, testifying to her strong visual aesthetic. 'I have switched my love of fashion into baking. I can spend two hours on one cake! I love cooking for a crowd.' Now, her greatest joy is preparing afternoon tea for her friends.

Spinach Soup

Potage aux Épinards

Served with a splash of cream, this soup has a velvety smooth texture. Try to avoid overcooking the spinach, as the soup will turn grey instead of green.

2 tablespoons canola oil

2 onions, finely chopped

2 stalks celery, finely chopped

2 large potatoes, finely chopped

2 litres (3½ pints) chicken stock

1 bunch spinach

salt

ground black pepper

cream

Heat oil in a saucepan and sauté the onions until soft and slightly browned. Add the celery, potatoes, stock and half the spinach. Cook until all the vegetables are softened, about 20 minutes. Add the remaining spinach and bring to the boil. Remove the saucepan from the heat and, once cool, purée in a food processor until smooth. Season to taste and serve with a splash of cream.

Serves 6

Asparagus with Eggs and Vinaigrette

Asperges aux Sauce Polonaise

1 bunch asparagus

2 slices white bread

2 hard-boiled eggs, finely chopped

DRESSING

80 ml (3 fl oz) olive oil

2 tablespoons red wine vinegar

1 teaspoon Dijon mustard

pinch of sugar

salt

ground black pepper

Preheat the oven to 180°C (350°F).

Chop 3 cm (1½ in) off the bottom of the asparagus spears and discard. Peel the stems with a vegetable peeler.

Fill a large frying pan with water and bring to the boil. Cook the asparagus until al dente, then remove from the pan and immediately rinse with cold water. (This method will retain the green colour of the asparagus.)

Crumble bread into fine crumbs. Toast in the oven until dry and lightly browned. Whisk together all the dressing ingredients.

Place asparagus on a plate, lightly dress with the vinaigrette, and garnish with the breadcrumbs and egg.

Serves 4

Red Wine Chicken Casserole

Coq au Vin

This is one of the oldest recipes in French provincial cuisine. The long simmering produces a rich and subtle blend. It is best made a day in advance to allow the flavours to be absorbed.

4 chicken Marylands or large drumsticks

2 tablespoons plain flour

3 tablespoons canola oil

4 spring onions or 1 onion, quartered

2 cups red wine

2 litres (3½ pints) chicken stock

6 small button mushrooms

1 tablespoon butter

1 squeeze lemon juice

1 bouquet garni

salt

ground black pepper

pickled onions (optional)

Preheat the oven to 170°C (340°F).

Roll the chicken pieces in flour. Heat the oil in a casserole dish and brown the chicken pieces. Add the spring onions and stir for a couple of minutes. Add the wine and stock to cover the chicken, and stir until well combined.

In a saucepan, cook the mushrooms in butter and lemon juice until they soften and brown slightly. Add the mushrooms and bouquet garni to the casserole dish. Place dish in the oven and cook, covered, for 1 hour, until the chicken is tender. Season to taste. Pickled onions may be tossed into the casserole before serving. Serve with mashed potato and green beans.

Serves 4

Chocolate Cake

Reine de Saba

This rich cake, coated in a chocolate ganache, forms part of Suzanne's extensive repertoire of desserts.

4 eggs, separated

185 g (6 oz) dark chocolate

185 g (6 oz) unsalted butter, chopped

185 g (6 oz) caster sugar

⅓ cup plain flour

pinch of salt

2 tablespoons ground almonds

1 teaspoon vanilla essence

CHOCOLATE GANACHE

230 ml (8 fl oz) thickened cream

185 g (6 oz) dark chocolate

Preheat the oven to 170°C (340°F).

Grease a 20 cm (8 in) springform cake tin and line the base with a circle of baking paper. Beat the egg whites until they form soft peaks. Melt the chocolate and butter in a bowl over a saucepan of boiling water. Remove and keep warm.

Beat the egg yolks and sugar until thick and lemon in colour. Add the chocolate mixture and slowly fold in the flour, salt, almonds and vanilla essence. With a metal spoon, fold in the egg whites. Pour mixture into the cake tin and bake for 1 hour.

Test with a toothpick – if it comes out dry, the cake is ready. Remove from the oven and place on a cake rack to cool.

To make the ganache, bring the cream to the boil in a saucepan. Melt the chocolate in a bowl over a saucepan of boiling water. Add to the cream and whisk until smooth. Cool until the mixture reaches a spreading consistency. Pour the ganache over the cake and smooth with a knife.

Serves 10

Opposite Reine de Saba

Fruit Tart

Tarte aux Fruits

CREME PATISSIERE

2 cups milk

¼ vanilla bean or 1 teaspoon vanilla essence

4 egg yolks

100 g (3½ oz) caster sugar

50 g (1½ oz) plain flour

SHORTCRUST PASTRY

375 g (14 oz) self-raising flour

220 g (8 oz) unsalted butter, chopped

60 g (2 oz) sugar

1 egg

FRUITS

1½ punnets strawberries, sliced

2 kiwi fruit, sliced

10 cherries, pitted and sliced

GLAZE

3 tablespoons apricot jam

Bring the milk and vanilla to the boil. In a double boiler, whisk the egg yolks and sugar until fluffy. Add the flour and whisk well. Remove the vanilla bean and pour the milk into the egg yolk mixture, stirring well. Return to the double boiler, stirring constantly until the mixture thickens to a custard. Remove from heat and transfer to a bowl. Cool, cover with plastic wrap and refrigerate until required.

To make the pastry, blend the flour, butter and sugar in a food processor until the mixture resembles breadcrumbs. Blend in the egg until the mixture forms a ball. Roll out the dough onto baking paper so that it is 1 cm (½ in) thick. Refrigerate for 20 minutes.

Preheat the oven to 180°C (350°F). Place the rolled dough in a 22 cm (8½ in) pastry flan and trim the edges. Allow some overhang, as pastry will shrink while cooking. Prick the base with a fork, line the pastry with baking paper or foil and fill with a layer of dried beans or rice and bake for 15–20 minutes, until pastry is golden brown.

To assemble, pour the chilled crème pâtissière into the cooled pastry shell and decorate with fruit. Heat the jam in a saucepan until it is runny, or for 1 minute in a microwave. Brush fruit with jam.

Serves 12

Concorde Cake

A Parisian pastry chef is said to have invented this cake in the early 1970s.
The crisp meringue and smooth mousse proved perfect companions.

MERINGUE

300 g (11 oz) icing sugar

⅓ cup cocoa

10 egg whites

300 g (11 oz) caster sugar

CHOCOLATE CREAM

500 ml (16 fl oz) thickened cream

125 g (4 oz) dark chocolate, melted and kept warm

1 teaspoon vanilla essence or rum

Preheat the oven to 150°C (300°F). To make the meringue, line three trays with baking paper. Sift the icing sugar and cocoa into a bowl. Beat egg whites separately until soft peaks form. Gradually add the caster sugar and beat well for about 3 minutes to form a firm meringue. Fold in the icing sugar and cocoa mixture.

Using a piping bag with a plain medium-sized nozzle, pipe three discs 22 cm (8½ in) in diameter. With the extra mixture, pipe 10 cm (4 in) logs onto baking paper and bake with the discs. Bake for about 45 minutes until firm to the touch. Leave to cool.

To make the chocolate cream, beat the cream until softly whipped. Add warm (but not hot) chocolate and vanilla, and beat until stiff.

To assemble the cake, place one meringue disc on a serving plate and spread with half the chocolate cream. Repeat and finish with last meringue. Sift icing sugar on top and decorate with extra logs of meringue.

Serves 10–12

Katalin Tyler HUNGARY

I don't cook from recipes. I use a little of this, a little of that. As I get older, I know the taste. Before the fast of Yom Kippur I don't prepare my best known dish, chicken paprika, as it is too salty. On the Sabbath, I cook my own nockedli just like my mother used to.

BORN in 1924 in a small Hungarian village called Berettyò-Ujfalu, approximately half a day's journey from Budapest, Katalin had a large extended family. Her father, Louis, was a butcher, while her mother, Helen, often worked in their busy store. Market days – Mondays and Thursdays – were frenetic as this was when all the locals would buy their week's supply of meat. Katalin's mother made delicious cabbage rolls in large portions, chicken paprika and noodles with cottage cheese. Since the family kept kosher, they often ate dairy. Cholent was prepared in advance for the Sabbath. On Saturday, this hearty dish was taken across to the Jewish baker to be baked in a slow oven throughout the night, absorbing a variety of flavours. Each family labelled their pot to distinguish the many vessels that arrived at the baker's for this longstanding tradition.

Although Katalin didn't cook with her mother, she remembers the dishes Helen lovingly prepared. On Sunday, she cooked pancakes with jam, nuts and sugar. On Rosh Hashanah she prepared goose and potatoes. She pickled her own cucumbers and cooked both chicken and veal schnitzels. Potatoes have always been a staple of Hungarian cuisine, sometimes served with sausages. Katalin clearly remembers her mother's delicious goulash.

Katalin attended a Jewish school, then a non-Jewish private school where there were two other Jewish girls in her class. As a teenager she enjoyed going to the swimming pool and to the movies in her village, and she completed her studies at the age of sixteen.

In 1944, when Katalin was nineteen, she and her parents were deported on a wagon to a ghetto in Romania. For a short time they lived in a filthy stable with scant food. After three weeks they were sent to Auschwitz. Upon arrival, Katalin was immediately separated from the others. All her family perished. Cramped in a block, the inmates received almost no food or water. One meal was provided every day – salami, cheese and bread. Their hair was shaved and they were perpetually dirty. Every morning, they endured the routine of being counted before returning to their cramped quarters. Ever resourceful, Katalin would swiftly jump through a window opening to find a space in the appalling living conditions in the block. Katalin remembers a large, ominous electric fence surrounding the compound.

Along with seventy-five girls from her village, Katalin began work in a cotton factory in Germany in oppressive conditions. Although she was starving, she worked all night, while German women

worked all day. Katalin and her co-workers were rounded up by the Germans and forced to trek and dig ditches until the war ended in May 1945. In freezing temperatures, Katalin slept in just a dress and coat. When liberated by the Russians, she was given semolina and milk to regain her strength, and a train ticket to Czechoslovakia. Remarkably, despite this bitter experience, Katalin says she always maintained optimism.

In June 1945, Katalin returned to her village in Hungary to search for any surviving family members and found her uncle and brother. While there, she met Ian, an accountant. They married in Budapest in 1946. At first, they lived together with Ian's three sisters. Eventually, Katalin's brother Steve married Ian's sister Martha in Vienna and Katalin and Ian moved to their own home in Budapest. Their two children – Judy and George – were born there. Katalin employed a lady who helped her with cooking while her husband worked in their small supermarket. In 1949, the young family left Hungary for Vienna, where many Jews came to seek migration permits to other countries. They lived in a hostel with shared facilities.

In 1950, the family arrived in Melbourne. Katalin was twenty-six and spoke no English. Ian wrote shopping lists for her in Hungarian, with an English translation he worked out from a dictionary. Ian soon found work at the Holden factory and quickly learned English. He then set up a shoemaking business with Katalin's brother Steve for about eighteen months. Ian started managing a boarding house in Brighton where the family lived for one year. A friend lent them money to lease another boarding house and the family was soon in a position to purchase a flat.

In 1982, Katalin's beloved husband died. She later married her brother-in-law, Joseph, whom she had met in Vienna. Joseph's first wife had fled abruptly, leaving their son and a note announcing her departure.

Katalin loves to cook cholent in winter as it is 'easy and tasty, with lovely flavours'. Its main ingredients are onions, garlic, soaked beans, potatoes, barley, smoked beef and paprika for colour. She still prepares goulash according to her mother's recipe of onions, fresh capsicum, paprika and veal. Each member of Katalin's family likes different dishes and she adores cooking for them, especially when her extended family visits for the weekly Sabbath meal on Friday nights. Katalin is famous for her chicken paprika accompanied by Hungarian spinach, and fresh fruit served for dessert: a delectable feast as family members joyfully gather around her table.

Katalin Tyler

Chicken and Vegetable Soup

Zöldség Leves

This soup is generally served at the Sabbath meal. The paprika gives it a vivid red colour.

1 tablespoon sunflower oil

1 onion, finely chopped

¼ red capsicum, finely chopped

2 cloves garlic, minced

1 teaspoon sweet paprika

3 carrots, chopped

4 stalks celery, finely chopped

3 potatoes, finely chopped

2 parsnips, finely chopped

2 chicken carcasses (frames)

2 chicken wings

2 chicken Marylands, halved

½ cauliflower, cut into small florets

½ broccoli, cut into small florets

1 cup frozen peas

1 vegetable stock cube

1 tablespoon salt

½ teaspoon ground black pepper

Heat the oil in a large saucepan and sauté the onion and capsicum for 3–4 minutes, or until softened. Stir through the garlic and paprika and then add the carrots, celery, potatoes, parsnips and chicken. Stir for a couple of minutes and cover with water. Cover the saucepan with a lid, bring to the boil and cook on a medium heat for 1½ hours. Add the cauliflower, broccoli, peas, stock, salt and pepper and cook for a further 30 minutes.

Serves 12–14

Mushrooms and Rice

Gombás Rizs

1 tablespoon vegetable oil

1 brown onion, finely chopped

500 g (1 lb) mushrooms, finely chopped

4 cups water

2 cups brown rice

1 teaspoon salt

¼ teaspoon ground black pepper

Heat the oil in a saucepan and sauté the onion until it browns slightly. Add the mushrooms, stirring regularly until they soften. In a separate saucepan, combine the water, rice and salt. Bring it to the boil and then simmer the rice on a low heat for about 20 minutes, until the water is absorbed and the rice cooked. Mix the rice with the mushrooms and onion, season to taste and serve.

Serves 8–10

Western Europe, Hungary

Opposite Chicken Paprika

Chicken Paprika

Csirke Paprikás

Katalin is famous for this piquant, quintessentially Hungarian dish.

1 chicken, skinned and cut into 8 pieces

3 tablespoons vegetable oil

1 onion, finely chopped

2 cloves garlic, minced

½ red capsicum, finely chopped

1 teaspoon salt

¼ teaspoon ground black pepper

1 teaspoon sweet paprika

Wash the chicken and pat it dry with paper towels. Heat the oil in a saucepan and sauté the onion, garlic and capsicum until they soften. Add the chicken, salt, pepper and paprika, and stir until the chicken is browned. Lower the heat, cover the saucepan and simmer for about 30 minutes, until the chicken is soft and a sauce has formed.

Serves 4

Katalin Tyler

Spinach

Spenot

1 kg (2 lb) frozen spinach, defrosted
1 tablespoon vegetable oil
2 tablespoons plain flour
1 clove garlic, minced
2 eggs, beaten
1 teaspoon salt

Drain the spinach. Heat the oil in a saucepan, add the flour and stir to make a paste. Add the garlic and spinach and stir for a few minutes until well combined. Gradually incorporate the eggs while stirring. Add salt to taste and simmer on moderate heat for 5 minutes.

Serves 8

Poppyseed Cake

Mákos Torta

The grated apple in this recipe makes the cake very moist.

10 eggs, separated
2 cups caster sugar
2 cups vegetable oil
4 golden delicious apples, peeled and grated
250 g (9 oz) ground poppy seeds
1 heaped teaspoon vanilla sugar
40 g (1½ oz) baking powder
80 g (3 oz) self-raising flour
250 g (9 oz) ground walnuts
icing sugar for dusting

Preheat the oven to 180°C (350°F).

Beat the egg yolks with sugar until pale, then add all the other ingredients, except the egg whites, and beat until well combined. Beat the egg whites until stiff, then gently fold them into the cake mixture.

Line a 35 cm x 25 cm (14 in x 10 in) baking tin with baking paper. Pour the mixture into the tin and bake for 1 hour. Cool and dust with icing sugar.

Serves 16

Opposite Poppyseed Cake

Perla Caviglia ITALY

On Sundays, I helped my mother cook so she could sleep in. Italian cooking uses good-quality, fresh ingredients: the easiest things, but you must prepare with your heart.

BORN in Rome in 1947, Perla Caviglia grew up in Via delle Carrozze with her older sister, Malka, and her younger sister, Sarah, in a Yiddish-speaking household. Their Polish father, Mendel (Manfredo), owned a lens factory while their Italian mother, Miriam Sarah, ran an optician's store. Originally, Perla's paternal grandfather, Mordechai Marco, had escaped from military service in Poland while his wife Elka was expecting their first son in Bychawa. Alone, Elka gave birth to Mendel and joined her husband in Germany. They then settled in the Italian town of Pieve di Cadore, Belluno – an area specialising in optical goods – near the famous resort Cortina. Eventually, they decided to relocate to Rome in order to set up a factory, which still exists today in Via dell'Orso.

Perla often stayed with her orthodox grandparents and every Sabbath Elka prepared gefilte fish and chicken soup for her many guests. Mordechai Marco built the Ashkenazi synagogue and was a chief of the Jewish community, helping people in transit before their migration. On the other side of her family, Perla's maternal grandfather was a famous fresco painter. As restrictions for Italian Jews intensified, Perla's grandparents went into hiding, changing residence every day, the risk greater as they couldn't speak Italian. Charismatic and handsome, Perla's father went to hide in the mountains with partisans and her mother would regularly take him food. He became an interpreter for an Italian general working for a German commander, pretending he was Armenian in order to survive.

Miriam Sarah loved to bake, especially her 'unbelievable walnut strudel', and prepared her own Passover wine with cherries and sugar stored all year in a large bottle. She made a combination of traditional Jewish food (such as kneidlach) and Italian dishes (like zabaglione) for their regular Sunday lunch. When Perla's older sister, Malka, was eight she was put in charge of the business while their parents were travelling for work. From the age of six, Perla was responsible for taking care of the home and in her zest for the task, she would get lost in the food stalls of the nearby market.

Since their mother liked 'beauty and elegance', Perla set their table carefully. After school and during holidays, the close-knit sisters worked in the lens factory cleaning dirty lenses with acetone: 'Hard work was always part of our lifestyle.' While her parents were busy working, a live-in nanny, Francesca, looked after Perla's baby sister, Sarah. A country girl, Francesca prepared panzanella by soaking old bread in water to soften it, then cooking it in oil, tomato and oregano like a bruschetta. There was a vegetable garden at the lens factory, so Perla brought home fresh produce for cooking.

At thirteen, Perla met Fabio at the Ben Akiva youth movement. Even though he was only fifteen, he wanted to become engaged to Perla as soon as he set eyes on her. He has been by her side ever since, especially when, as a teenager, she was gravely ill with rheumatic fever and had to stay in bed for

eighteen months. After a five-year engagement, when Perla was twenty, the young couple married in Rome and opened a fashion store. Perla prides herself on traditional family values of devotion and togetherness. In 1969, when Perla was pregnant with their first child, her mother died of cancer and her father married a Libyan woman who worked at the Hebrew Immigrant Aid Society.

Perla's mother-in-law, Rina, became a strong influence as the family holidayed together in Monte Porzio, near Frascati. A strong woman who was widowed, 'she was always behind me; there when I needed it.' Fabio struggled with the unfamiliar flavours of Ashkenazi food: 'Every Sabbath was a drama because he wouldn't touch anything. He would eat sandwiches beforehand.' Rina helped Perla prepare delicious, fresh yet simple Italian dishes such as pomodori con riso or concia.

Rina and her two sisters are the only survivors from her family. In 1942, the Nazis went to the main piazza in Rome, near the synagogue, and took everyone away. Rina used to read recipes from her cookbook in order to compensate for starvation during the war. In a loving gesture just before their move to Australia, Rina gave Perla her valuable book, which has become a lucky talisman.

Roman Jewish cuisine is seasonal, with artichokes and peas prepared during spring and lamb for Passover. On Rosh Hashanah, rice is served because the many tiny grains are symbolic of luck, while a whole fish such as mullet is presented with the head intact to include the brain for knowledge. Rina taught Perla to prepare pasta with freshly grated parmigiana, cooked at the last minute while guests wait eagerly at the table. Perla cooks with 'whatever is in the house'.

In 1974, Perla and Fabio, along with their sons, Pacifico and Alessio, visited Australia for a holiday. Six months later they decided to migrate to Melbourne: they had discovered 'paradise'. Concerned about rising anti-Semitism in Rome, Perla and Fabio were increasingly frightened to declare their Jewish identity and longed for a safer environment for their children. Initially, they lived partly in Rome and partly in Melbourne but eventually they settled permanently in Australia where the community was extremely welcoming – 'all the doors were open'. In 1995, the family moved to Sydney to enjoy a warmer climate and a casual, Mediterranean-type lifestyle.

Wherever they live, Perla takes her precious family photos with her: 'My photos are like my home. Jewish people make a home anywhere in the world. We all speak the same language. We all have common bonds even if we are different nationalities.'

Now, Perla's daughters-in-law cook Italian food in their Sydney homes. Perla continues to be inspired by her mother's elegant aesthetic. She sets her Sabbath table with special silver and crystal glasses and each dish is served on its own plate so as not to confuse flavours: the table gleams with beauty. On Sundays, she loves to bake with her grandson, Fabio, while a fresh penne is cooking in the oven.

Western Europe, Italy

Tomatoes Stuffed with Rice

Pomodori con Riso

Stuffed tomatoes are a universal dish and rice is one of the most common fillings.
This particular version is Roman.

9 large vine-ripened tomatoes

2 cloves garlic

180 g (6 oz) arborio rice

1 heaped tablespoon salt

100 ml (3½ fl oz) extra virgin olive oil

9 basil leaves

6 large potatoes, quartered

olive oil

sea salt

Preheat the oven to 200°C (400°F).

Slice the tops off the tomatoes, retaining them to use as lids. Scoop out the flesh of the tomatoes and blend with garlic in a food processor until puréed. Pour the purée into a bowl with the rice, salt and olive oil, mixing well. Spoon the filling evenly into the cavities of the tomatoes, place a basil leaf on top of each and close with the tomato lid. Stand the tomatoes in an ovenproof dish, with the potatoes interspersed between them. Drizzle tomatoes and potatoes with olive oil and sprinkle with sea salt. Bake for 45 minutes and serve hot.

Serves 9

Penne with Béchamel Sauce

Penne al Gratin

This pasta dish is baked in a creamy white sauce.

500 g (1 lb) penne

SAUCE

185 g (6 oz) butter

3 tablespoons plain flour

1.5 litres (2½ pints) milk

pinch of sea salt

150 g (5 oz) parmesan cheese

Preheat the oven to 200°C (400°F).

Melt the butter in a saucepan, then remove from heat. Stir through the flour until a smooth paste forms. Add a little milk and stir until smooth and well combined. Pour in the remaining milk and heat on low, stirring continuously until the sauce thickens. Remove from heat and allow to cool. Add the salt and cheese, and stir.

Cook the penne in boiling salted water until al dente, about 10 minutes. Drain the pasta, combine with the béchamel sauce and pour into a greased oven dish. Bake for 30–40 minutes, until golden brown. Serve hot.

Serves 4–6

Fusilli with Fresh Tomato Sauce

Pasta Fredda

This quick pasta dish uses fresh tomatoes, garlic and basil. It is a great summer dish served cold.

500 g (1 lb) fusilli

SAUCE

8 Roma tomatoes, skinned, deseeded and chopped

3 cloves garlic

160 ml (5½ fl oz) olive oil

1 teaspoon salt

8 basil leaves

Place the tomatoes in a bowl with the garlic, oil, salt and basil. Leave the ingredients to rest for half an hour to allow the flavours to infuse.

Cook the fusilli in boiling salted water until al dente, about 10 minutes. Drain the pasta and add the sauce. Mix, cool and serve.

Serves 4–6

Farfalle with Vodka

Farfalle alla Vodka

A nice creamy tomato sauce with a kick.

500 g (1 lb) farfalle

handful of basil leaves

SAUCE

80 ml (3 fl oz) olive oil

1 onion, halved

2 cloves garlic

750 ml sugo

50 ml (1½ fl oz) vodka

pinch of salt

300 ml (11 fl oz) cream

50 g (1½ oz) Parmesan cheese, grated

Heat the oil in a saucepan and add the onion and garlic. Stir for a minute to allow the flavours to combine, then discard the onion and garlic. Add the sugo and cook on a high heat for 10–15 minutes. Add the vodka, and stir the sauce for 2–3 minutes to allow the alcohol to evaporate. Let the sauce simmer over a low heat for 10 minutes. Add the salt and cream, and remove from heat after a few seconds.

Cook the farfalle in boiling salted water until al dente, about 10 minutes, then drain.

Add the parmesan to the sauce and mix it through the pasta. Garnish with whole basil leaves.

Serves 4–6

Italian Meat Loaf

Polpettone di Pollo

Challah crumbs may be substituted for breadcrumbs.

6 skinless chicken breast fillets, minced

2 cups fresh breadcrumbs

2 eggs, beaten

pinch of salt

2 hard-boiled eggs, peeled

120 ml (4½ fl oz) olive oil

2 carrots

1 cup white wine

Mix the chicken, breadcrumbs, beaten eggs and salt in a bowl. With moist hands, mould the mixture into a loaf, and place the hard-boiled eggs into the centre. Heat the oil in a casserole dish on the stove. Add the meat loaf and brown each side, taking care to maintain the shape. Add the carrots and wine to the casserole dish, and enough water to cover the loaf.

Cover the dish with a lid or foil and cook on a medium heat for 30 minutes. Mash the carrots in the dish to make a sauce and serve.

Serves 8–10

Scotch Fillet with Green Pea Sauce

Spezzatino con Piselli

120 ml (4½ fl oz) olive oil

1 onion, finely sliced

1.5 kg (3 lb) Scotch fillet, chopped

1 cup white wine

1 kg (2 lb) peas, shelled

salt

ground black pepper

Heat the oil in a saucepan and sauté the onion until softened. Add the meat and cook on a high heat until browned. Pour the wine over the meat and stir for 2–3 minutes to allow the alcohol to evaporate. Add water to cover and cook for 20 minutes, covered, on a medium heat. Add the peas, cover and cook for a further 20–30 minutes, until the peas are soft and the sauce has reduced.

Serves 8–10

Zucchini Antipasto

Concia

This makes a great vegetarian antipasto.

2 kg (4 lb) zucchini
250 ml (9 fl oz) olive oil
2 cloves garlic
6 basil leaves
olive oil

Wash and pat the zucchini dry with paper towels, then cut them diagonally into 5 cm (2 in) thick pieces. Heat the oil in a wok or deep frying pan. Fry the zucchini in batches until golden brown, making sure to turn them only once so that they don't fall apart.

Put the fried zucchini in a dish with the whole garlic cloves and basil leaves. Drizzle with olive oil and serve hot or at room temperature.

Serves 8–10

Pears in Red Wine

Pere al Vino Rosso

4 cups water
4 cups Kiddush wine (sweet red wine)
90 g (3 oz) sugar
1 teaspoon ground cinnamon
6 firm brown pears, peeled

In a saucepan combine the water, wine, sugar and cinnamon. Place the pears in the pan and boil, covered, until the liquid thickens, about 15 minutes. Uncover and boil for a further 15 minutes. Pears should be soft without losing their shape. Serve at room temperature.

Serves 6

Peaches with Lemon

Pesche al Limone

8 peaches

90 g (3 oz) sugar

juice of 2 lemons

Peel peaches and slice into thin wedges. Add sugar and lemon juice and allow to rest for half an hour before serving.

Serves 6

Strawberries with Balsamic Vinegar

Fragole con Aceto Balsamico

A light and refreshing way to end a meal.

1 kg (2 lb) strawberries

90 g (3 oz) sugar

1 tablespoon balsamic vinegar

Slice the strawberries into halves or quarters, depending on their size, then mix them with the sugar and vinegar. Allow to rest for half an hour before serving.

Serves 6–8

Western Europe, Italy

Hazel Shapiro SCOTLAND

When there was nothing left in the house, my mother would make conglomeration pie – odds and ends such as beaten eggs and a tin of spaghetti assembled into a delicious pie. This is one of my fondest childhood memories. Our family was very poor but sometimes exquisite meals were prepared from the simplest of means.

HAZEL Shapiro uses two cherished cookbooks – *Jewish Cookery* by Leah H. Leonard (1951) and *Lofty Peak* (1977), full of Scottish sweet and savoury baking recipes. Given to her by her beloved mother, these books encapsulate the disparate influences on her unique cuisine – the wholesome, hearty food of Scotland, with its uncomplicated cooking style, contrasted with traditional Jewish dishes. Hazel regularly prepares beef steak pie and sausage rolls just like her mother, as well as tweed kettle – a kind of poached salmon. Both cuisines consist of home-style – *hamish* – cooking, with the most essential ingredient being 'the bringing of pleasure and enjoyment to people's faces'.

Born in Edinburgh in 1948, Hazel is one of six children. Her mother, Yetta, was English, her father, William (a taxi driver), was Scottish. The couple met when William was on leave from the army and passed her on the street. Entranced, they married soon after. Originally from Lodz, Yetta's family had migrated to England in 1904. As orthodox Jews, they partly disowned her when she married a non-Jewish man. During World War II, Hazel's father was absent for five years as a member of the British army. His family were religious Christians and Hazel attended Sunday School conducted by her two devout aunts. Hazel's mother intervened and ceased the classes when Hazel was nine.

Yetta was a talented dressmaker by trade but she was an 'average cook, barely able to boil an egg. Her mother did everything for her.' Nevertheless, Hazel and her siblings enjoyed typical English food such as toad in the hole, shepherd's pie and Yorkshire pudding. Growing up in a housing commission area called The Inch, Hazel and her siblings attended the local schools. Their cramped, two-storey house accommodated the family of eight and Hazel shared a room with her twin sisters, Carol and Linda.

Hazel had 'no idea' that she was Jewish but recalls anti-Semitic taunts at school and a derogatory skipping rope rhyme chanted by the children. When Hazel eventually asked her mother about their identity, the sensitive topic was avoided. Yet Hazel always felt attached to her mother as she was 'very intelligent – all my friends loved her and enjoyed meeting her.' Hazel recalls having one Jewish friend, Cynthia Reif, who was in her sister's class.

In 1961, the family migrated to Australia in an attempt to improve their quality of life, as conditions in Scotland were arduous for a mother of six children. Hazel's oldest sister, Sheila, remained in Edinburgh, where she married and staunchly rejected their Jewish heritage. Hazel's parents, referred to as 'ten-pound migrants', paid the budget ticket price for the four-week journey through the Suez Canal to Australia. 'Our lives were turned upside-down coming to Australia,' Hazel recalls. 'It was just another traumatic event.' Hazel was twelve and a half, and her sisters Linda and Carol not quite fourteen, when they arrived in their new country.

Initially planning to settle in Adelaide, Yetta had met a gentleman on the ship called Jack Gordon, who convinced her that there was a flourishing Jewish community in Melbourne. Upon arrival, the family lived for two weeks at the Exhibition Buildings before they were allocated to a migrant hostel. Hazel attended Preston Girls' High School and then a technical college until the end of 1961. School uniforms were too expensive to send her sisters as well, so instead they went to work with their mother at the Hycraft clothing factory.

The family moved into a rented house in Heidelberg. Hazel's father started work as a tram driver while her mother found employment as a machinist at a men's suit factory. One of the factory workers, Harry Meyer, suggested that Yetta join Kew synagogue, where she started attending services on high holy days as well keeping a kosher home. Hazel remembers: 'It was confusing for us. Our friends at Habonim Youth Movement were from the Jewish day school, Mount Scopus. They were affluent and didn't accept us, looking down on us because we were poor and working.' Having spent numerous years devoid of Jewish identity, Hazel's mother, however, seemed to rejoice in her newfound freedom.

In 1963, the family moved to Malvern when the rented home of some friends became vacant. Renee and Alan Shapero from England suggested they take up their lease and Hazel was all in favour – she 'always loved the name Shapiro, especially the singer Helen Shapiro'. It was to be an omen.

The week after Hazel turned fourteen, she finished school in order to care for her younger siblings – 'cooking, cleaning and taking them to school' – as well as making the beds, running the household and, on one occasion, even putting out a hedge fire. Her mother started work at 7 a.m. and would give instructions for what to prepare for meals – burgers, potatoes, peas – 'simple fare'.

At the age of fifteen, Hazel worked at a cake shop, then at another bakery. She was fascinated by the baking methods and her lifelong passion for food was ignited. She left the bakery to work in a clothing factory producing men's pyjamas and shirts, and later in an office where she was sent to learn accountancy on 'a machine like a gigantic typewriter: a precursor to the computer'. But she retained the memory of food.

One night, Hazel and her close friend, Wendy, went out to a dance at Sergio's, on the Esplanade in St Kilda. It was a predominantly Jewish gathering and that night both Hazel and Wendy met their prospective husbands – in Hazel's case an Israeli by the name of Sam Shapiro. Sam worked at a men's clothing factory called Jedwab & Co. Hazel married her sweetheart in 1970, welcoming their first child, Ruth, in 1974. Tammy, Elana and Zvi followed.

Hazel's mother-in-law, Batsheva, has been her main source of inspiration in the kitchen. Visiting her daily, Hazel avidly watched her cook for Rosh Hashanah – delicious Sephardi and Israeli dishes. 'She cooked from memory: a handful of this, a handful of that. I used to call her to verify recipes, as they were often inexact.' Batsheva prepared food with tremendous variety and supreme effort. From her, Hazel learned to cook traditional dishes such as gefilte fish, chopped liver and cholent. On one occasion, Hazel's mother cooked for her in-laws, preparing gefilte fish from frozen ingredients. 'It was a disaster and broke my heart on her behalf.'

Hazel Shapiro

POULTRY

In 1989, at the age of seventy-three, Hazel's mother fell into a coma. Hazel kept a bedside vigil, barely leaving her mother's side. She asked her mother to give her a sign. Yetta opened her eyes and focused on Hazel, then sighed and died in peace. Hazel cherishes this final connection.

From 1991, for eight years, Hazel ran the canteen at Yavneh College, surrounded by children and immersed in a Jewish environment. She recalls these as the most blissful years of her life. Since 1991, she has been an active member of Melbourne's Elsternwick synagogue, co-ordinating catering and preparing menus for Kiddushim and the delicious Chanukah barbecue.

Divorced in 1992, Hazel remains proud of her four children, to whom she is devoted. Her frenetic life revolves around their wellbeing while she works with her son, Zvi, at a kosher butcher. Her daughter Tammy is a talented pastry chef capable of baking intricate croquembouche, Ruth is a dispensary technician in a pharmacy and Elana works in London. Hazel's grandson, Jacob, comes every Friday night for the Sabbath feast, his little hands savouring challah, kneidlach and even Dundee cake.

Scotch Broth

Mutton was a frequent ingredient in Scottish meals and, when Scotch broth was brewing, the mutton would often be used as the main course, rather than being chopped up and returned to the pot. To make a parve version of this soup, omit the lamb shanks and add 2 tablespoons of Vegemite or Marmite.

2 lamb shanks

3.5 litres (6 pints) water

80 g (3 oz) pearl barley

4 large carrots, finely chopped

1 large onion, finely chopped

1 parsnip, finely chopped

1 small turnip, finely chopped

3 potatoes, finely chopped

2 stalks celery, finely sliced

1 zucchini, finely sliced

18 green beans, cut into 2 cm (¾ in) pieces

1 head broccoli, including stem, cut into small pieces

3 onion stock cubes or 3 tablespoons onion soup mix

salt

ground black pepper

½ bunch parsley, finely chopped

Trim any excess fat from the lamb shanks and place them in a large saucepan with the water, vegetables and stock cubes. Bring to the boil and simmer on a low heat for 2 hours.

Remove the shanks from the saucepan and cut the meat into small pieces. Return the pieces to the saucepan, discarding the bone. Skim off any froth or fat that comes to the surface. Season to taste and garnish with parsley before serving.

Serves 6–8

Tweed Kettle

This dish is sometimes called salmon hash and was popular in Edinburgh in the nineteenth century.

1 kg (2 lb) salmon, preferably from tail end

1 teaspoon salt

¼ teaspoon ground white pepper

pinch of ground nutmeg

150 ml (5 fl oz) dry white wine

2 spring onions or 1 tablespoon chives, finely chopped

1 tablespoon parsley, finely chopped

Place the salmon in a saucepan, cover it with water and bring to the boil. Simmer gently on a low heat for 5 minutes, then remove the salmon, reserving the stock. Remove the skin and bones and cut the fish into 5 cm (2 in) squares. Season with salt, pepper and nutmeg and place in a saucepan with the wine and spring onions and 150 ml (5 fl oz) of the stock. Cover and simmer on a low heat for about 20 minutes. Serve hot or cold, and garnish with chopped parsley.

Serves 6–8

Scotch Eggs

*Here is a simple recipe for making a traditional Scottish dish which is still popular
served either hot or cold at picnics.*

5 hard-boiled eggs, peeled

2 tablespoons plain flour

¼ teaspoon ground nutmeg or mace

1 teaspoon salt

½ teaspoon ground black pepper

500 g (1 lb) sausage meat

1 large egg, beaten

1 tablespoon cold water

100 g (3½ oz) breadcrumbs

vegetable oil for frying

Dust the hard-boiled eggs in flour and shake off excess. Mix the nutmeg, salt and pepper with the sausage meat and divide into five equal portions. Place each portion on a floured surface and wrap around an egg, making sure there are no gaps.

Mix the egg and water, coat each meat-covered egg with the mixture, and then roll them in breadcrumbs. You may need to press the breadcrumbs onto the meat.

Deep-fry the eggs in medium to hot oil for about 10 minutes, until golden brown. Drain on paper towels, and serve hot with vegetables or cold as a snack.

Makes 5

Caledonian Cream

*A refreshing dessert which uses marmalade – a popular ingredient in Scottish cooking
since its invention in Dundee in 1797. It is best eaten within a few hours of preparation, as
refrigerating for too long will cause the cream to lose its texture.*

2 oranges, pith removed

1 teaspoon rum or whisky (optional)

rind of 2 oranges

CREAM

250 g (9 oz) cream cheese

250 ml (9 fl oz) double cream

2 tablespoons marmalade

2 tablespoons whisky or rum

2 teaspoons lemon juice

2 tablespoons caster sugar

Blend all the cream ingredients until smooth.

Segment the oranges and place in the bottom of four long-stemmed glasses. Add the rum to the oranges and pour the cream on top. Refrigerate until set.

Boil the orange rind in water for a few minutes to reduce the bitterness and then drain. Slice the rind and use to garnish the dessert before serving.

Serves 4

Opposite Scotch Eggs

Dundee Cake

A rich, fruity cake, this became popular at the end of the nineteenth century.
The whisky may be omitted or replaced with another spirit.

220 g (8 oz) butter or margarine

220 g (8 oz) brown sugar

2 teaspoons black treacle

1 tablespoon whisky or rum (optional)

6 eggs

30 g (1oz) ground almonds

300 g (11 oz) plain flour

30 g (1 oz) self-raising flour

100 g (3½ oz) chopped mixed peel

250 g (9 oz) sultanas

250 g (9 oz) currants

250 g (9 oz) raisins

milk

Preheat the oven to 160°C (320°F). Grease and line a 23 cm (9 in) round cake tin.

Cream the butter, sugar, treacle and whisky until light and fluffy. Add the eggs one at a time, mixing well as you go. Stir through the almonds, add the sieved flours and partly mix before adding the peel and dried fruits. Mix lightly but thoroughly until the batter is smooth. If mixture is too stiff, add a little milk to soften.

Pour mixture into the cake tin, covering it with baking paper to prevent burning. Bake near the middle of the oven for 2½–3 hours, removing baking paper about 20 minutes before cake is finished. Test with a toothpick – if the cake is still wet in the middle return it to the oven for further baking. Allow it to rest for 15 minutes before removing the cake from the tin and placing it on a wire rack. Cool and serve.

Serves 12

Middle East
Iraq, Israel, Lebanon

Sephardi Jews have lived in Middle Eastern and Arab countries since the late fifteenth century after being expelled from Spain. At its heart, Sephardi cooking has the warm undertones of Spain: it is olive oil based; rich with fish from the sea and the vegetables of a warm climate; and fragrant with garlic and herbs. Nuts, dried fruit and aromatic spices accompany many dishes, contributing interesting textures and flavours. Mezze provides an opportunity for sensuous and colourful presentation, with numerous salads and dips embellishing the table. Stuffed vegetables and rice are also part of the elaborate Middle Eastern culinary repertoire.

Nita Jawary IRAQ

Middle East

> *There is a little Baghdad in my home,* with the smells,
> traditions and values of a Jewish Iraqi home.
> Prepared with joy and abandon, as well as a
> keen understanding of the combination of
> ingredients, I cook from memory.

FOOD is the centre of an Iraqi Jewish home. Even though Nita Jawary was born in Melbourne, her home is abundant with the smells and spices of Iraq. Nita's mother, Sabiha, was married by proxy, by the Chief Rabbi of Baghdad, to her father who was living in Melbourne. The two had not previously met. The arranged marriage allowed Nita's mother to migrate to Australia in 1949.

Nita's mother and her aunt, Saud Feniger, are her main creative and culinary influences. Nita remembers her mother's cooking being suffused with artistic flair as she prepared a delicious weekly menu. Her aunt Saud 'put her life's energy into cooking for her family', especially for her two daughters, their husbands and her five grandchildren. Nita would watch her aunt bake intricate delicacies – there was always something 'warm and exquisite' on the table. Whenever she visited Nita with her children, Saud arrived with 'an open hand and an open heart'.

A source of health, happiness and family unity, cooking is a time-consuming endeavour for Iraqi women. Few of them use recipes, because Iraqi cooking is part of an oral tradition. Nita has collected some recipes from members of the Sephardi Association as well as a few family recipes that have become treasures: 'The beauty of cooking is not to use recipes. It is better to cook with love and warmth rather than duty. If you respect ingredients, it will come out beautiful.'

Cooking has traditionally been a communal activity for Iraqi women, huddled around tables chopping vegetables, mixing spices and preparing meat. Kitchens were often large in order to accommodate this flurry of activity that brought women together before the heat of the tanur (a large clay oven), exchanging advice and anecdotes.

Greens, salads and pickles accompany most meals, with vegetables the basis of all dishes. Summer heralds a profusion of greens: parsley, mint and basil add freshness to the table, suggesting regeneration, health and growth. There is a strong link between food and health in Iraqi culture. Spices are added to enhance the flavours of these fresh ingredients. Nita grows her own herbs and uses spices carefully: 'They mustn't overwhelm other flavours'.

When Nita was first married, she replicated what she had observed in her childhood home, becoming absorbed in the pleasures of cooking. Cumin and turmeric are the basis of many dishes, often modified according to the tastes of various family members. Rice is a staple of most meals. In Iraq, every Jewish girl was taught how to remove the sinew from lamb. Nita vividly recalls her

grandmother filling the intestines of lamb with rice, cardamom, cloves and chopped giblets: a dish she has never attempted. Following strict Kashrut laws and a Jewish lifestyle, her family prepared tebeet: chicken stuffed with short-grain rice, rose petals, chopped giblets and cinnamon. Her mother still makes this dish for Saturday lunch.

An artist, journalist, writer and marriage celebrant, Nita relishes the abundance, sensuality and colour of Iraqi food. She loves cooking a beetroot stew with meat dumplings in a rice-flour dough. The deep purple hue of beetroot is just one of the many vibrant colours that embellish her table. She often paints different ingredients and her home is filled with canvases and drawings. A mother of three, for her, 'art nourishes the soul and food nourishes the body'. Although her grandmother couldn't read or write, she was skilled at many artistic enterprises such as cooking and crocheting. Nita's artistic flair – like that of her mother and grandmother – infiltrates every aspect of her life.

In Iraq, Muslims cook with ghee while Jews cook with oil, in particular sesame oil. A water jug perfumed with a few drops of rosewater is provided with meals for washing hands. Food is presented banquet-, or mezze-, style with a variety of dishes on the table. There is great variety in Iraqi cuisine: dates on their stems, cardamom for Turkish coffee, fresh mint tea and brown eggs cooked overnight. Even the humblest dishes with basic ingredients can be fare for a king. In order to 'feed the eyes and feed the ears', meals are often accompanied by music, usually from the Arabic lute, the ud. Someone in Nita's family always played the ud, ensuring that meals were a time of rejoicing and festivity.

Sharing a meal with loved ones underpins Iraqi cuisine: 'One mustn't eat alone: good company and laughter must accompany every meal. Food is the focus of family. It is a way of showing love and receiving love.' Although produce and flavours are different in Australia, Nita continues her Iraqi tradition of preparing a variety of dishes for her table: it is resplendent with magnificent food, with the Sabbath 'the queen of all meals'.

Opposite Cauliflower and Aniseed (Fennel) Salad

Flat Bread with Cumin Seeds

Chubiz

1 cup plain flour

1 cup warm water

½ teaspoon salt

½ teaspoon ground black pepper

1 tablespoon cumin seeds

2 tablespoons flat-leaf parsley, finely chopped

1 tablespoon olive oil

Mix the flour, water, salt and pepper in a bowl until they form a moist dough. Mix in cumin seeds, parsley and olive oil. Leave to rest for half an hour.

Preheat the grill to 250°C (500°F). Take 3 tablespoons of dough and flatten into a disc. Repeat with the rest of the dough. Evenly space the chubiz on a hot oven tray. (Ensure the tray is hot to avoid the dough sticking.) Grill until golden brown.

Makes 4

Cauliflower and Aniseed (Fennel) Salad

¼ cauliflower, cut into small florets

½ fennel, cut horizontally into fine slices

1 tablespoon cumin seeds or ½ teaspoon ground cumin

1 tablespoon olive oil

1 tablespoon lemon juice

2 tablespoons flat-leaf parsley, finely chopped

Mix all ingredients and serve.

Serves 6

Onion Rice

2 cups water

½ teaspoon salt

¼ teaspoon ground black pepper

2 cups basmati rice, washed

80 ml (3 fl oz) olive oil

4 onions, finely sliced

½ bunch coriander, finely chopped

Pour the water in a saucepan, add salt and pepper and bring to the boil. Then add the rice. Once water returns to the boil, cover and simmer on a low heat for 20 minutes, until cooked, then transfer to serving dish.

Heat the oil in a frying pan and sauté the onions on a low heat until light brown. Arrange the fried onion on top of the rice and garnish with coriander.

Serves 8–10

Stuffed Tomatoes

Stuffed vegetables are a common side dish served at Iraqi banquets.

10 firm tomatoes

3 tablespoons plain flour

1 egg, beaten

2 tablespoons olive oil

SAUCE

½ tablespoon sugar

2 tablespoons lemon juice

1 teaspoon salt

1 teaspoon ground black pepper

FILLING

500 g (1 lb) minced lamb

1 large onion, finely chopped

2 cups continental parsley, finely chopped

½ teaspoon ground turmeric

½ teaspoon salt

¼ teaspoon ground black pepper

Cut the tops off the tomatoes and scoop out the flesh. Chop the tops and flesh.

To make the sauce, blend the chopped tomatoes in a food processor with the sugar, lemon juice, salt and pepper. Set aside.

To make the filling, mix the lamb, onion, parsley, turmeric, salt and pepper.

Stuff the tomato cavities with the filling, and coat the upper half of the tomatoes first with flour and then with egg.

Heat the oil in a deep frying pan and fry the tomatoes, face down, on a low heat for 5 minutes. Transfer the tomatoes to a saucepan and spoon the sauce around the stuffed tomatoes. Cover and simmer on a low heat for half an hour.

Serves 10

Opposite (clockwise from left) Beetroot Stew, Stuffed Tomatoes and Onion Rice

Beetroot Stew

Kibba Shuandi

This is a classic Iraqi stew made with kibba – small meat dumplings encased in a rice-flour dough.

STEW

1 tablespoon olive oil

2 onions, finely chopped

5 tomatoes, finely chopped

5 large beetroot, peeled and chopped

½ tablespoon sugar

½ teaspoon salt

½ teaspoon ground black pepper

2 teaspoons tamarind or lemon juice or pomegranate syrup

KIBBA

1 cup rice flour

¾ cup water

FILLING

1 cup minced lamb

1 onion, finely chopped

1 cup flat-leaf parsley, finely chopped

1 tablespoon ground turmeric

¼ teaspoon salt

¼ teaspoon ground black pepper

To make the stew, heat the oil in a deep saucepan and sauté the onions on a medium heat until softened. Add the tomatoes, beetroot and sugar, season with salt and pepper and simmer for 15 minutes on a low heat.

To make the kibba, mix the rice flour and water to make a dough. Additional flour or water may be required to achieve the correct consistency.

To make the filling, mix the lamb with the onion, parsley, turmeric, salt and pepper in a bowl. Moisten hands and take 1 tablespoon of the dough in the palm of your hand. Place ½ teaspoon of the filling in the middle of the dough and work the dough to surround the filling.

Drop the kibba into the simmering stew and leave them to cook for 10 minutes. Add the tamarind juice and serve with steamed basmati rice.

Serves 6

Yaffa Barak ISRAEL

Cooking is like art. You need to play with your imagination and logic – you can make it spicy or less spicy.

BORN in the Israeli seaside town of Haifa in 1956, Yaffa is the youngest of eight children, the only one not born in Morocco. Her mother, Marcel, was from Meknes, known as the 'European city of Morocco', while her father, Haviv, was a fisherman from Casablanca. His father (Yaffa's grandfather) owned a spice and dried fruit shop and remarried after Haviv's mother died during childbirth. Haviv had a troubled relationship with his stepmother and on one occasion, at the age of six, he threw a plate at her forehead during an argument. Fearful of repercussions, he fled and hid in a fishing boat. Gradually, he learned the trade while living with the fisherman. Although he never studied, he could speak French, Italian, Spanish, Portuguese and Arabic.

For years, the family searched for him in vain. At fourteen, he became the owner of the fishing boat and returned to Casablanca to buy spices. While walking down the street he accidentally stepped on someone's foot and a fight erupted. Strong and burly from years at sea, Haviv beat the other man, then entered the spice shop. The owner of the shop looked at him in disbelief, telling him that his victim was, in fact, his brother. Soon after, Haviv's father arrived, jubilant to see his lost son but worried that he might flee again. He swiftly resolved to find him a bride and Haviv was soon engaged to Marcel, a twelve-year-old girl from a wealthy, educated family.

Marcel's father had died when she was nine, so she started working as a housekeeper and live-in nanny. But her mother took all her earnings when she returned home on Saturdays. One day, Marcel arrived home to discover neighbours busily preparing a party. She was quickly dressed in a festive caftan and the celebrations for her engagement began. Marcel was downcast because she didn't understand what was unfolding around her. Many Jewish girls were kidnapped by Arabs because of their beauty. As a result, it was common for girls to be engaged from a young age to avoid being wrenched from their families. Marcel and Haviv settled in Casablanca; Marcel was pregnant at the age of fourteen while her husband continued his successful fishing business.

The couple had seven children when they were warned that Hitler would invade Morocco. With many Jews frightened, the family fled to France. Six years later, in 1954, they migrated to Israel. Initially, they lived in a tent as there were no buildings but they soon moved to a tin shack in Carmel. In Israel life was difficult for Jews from Arab countries: they were the 'black sheep' of the family.

When Yaffa was born, her mother was taken to a psychiatric hospital for shock treatment after the birth. During her pregnancy, she suffered from severe trauma because she had to identify the remains of her brother, who was hijacked and killed by Syrians while he was on a boat in the Kineret with a friend. With no Hebrew, Haviv was lost, working hard on building roads. Strong Zionists, Marcel and

Haviv had dreamed all their lives of settling in Israel with their large family, but the reality fell far short of their dream.

Marcel was a constant guide to her children, always maintaining a positive outlook. 'I never tasted food like hers,' Yaffa marvels. 'She could take simple ingredients like potatoes and you would think we were eating a king's meal.' She never repeated the same dish, ensuring there was tremendous variety in her cooking despite not having a fridge. Haviv and Marcel were devoted to each other. Yaffa remembers her father's love for her mother expressed through their 'special language with their eyes'. He was protective and adoring, and every Thursday he would bring home the groceries so Marcel didn't have to carry the parcels. He would shell peas and peel potatoes and carrots to help prepare for the Sabbath banquet.

Marcel would bake challah, cakes and biscuits in her clay oven for the many neighbours and guests who shared this feast. She also prepared cholent, stuffed chickens, lamb, vegetables stuffed with dried fruit and more than twenty salads and dips. Their door was always open, even for strangers who got lost on their journey. Marcel never wasted anything. With 'taste in her hands', she prepared marmalade from orange peel; chilli sauce; and her own olives and pickles. On Yom Kippur, to break the fast, she baked star-shaped bread with almonds and such spices as saffron and aniseed for extra flavour.

The family lived in a very old house from the Turkish era in Bat-Galim, Haifa – an Algerian, Moroccan and Tunisian neighbourhood. When Yaffa's older sister wanted to marry a soldier at the age of seventeen, her father vehemently disapproved. Miraculously, Marcel organised their wedding in one day while the men were out fishing. She purchased a five-tiered cake and arranged a photographer while Yaffa went to the market with her brothers, David and Avram, to buy live chickens for the celebration. Marcel prepared the entire banquet while the other children were sent out to invite the guests. Yaffa's brothers and their friends played exultant music and Marcel worked tirelessly from dawn to ensure that her daughter had a lavish wedding.

When Yaffa was on leave from the army, she went to the beach and Marcel arrived with two coolers full of food for family and friends. There, Yaffa was introduced to Sam, who was transfixed. After failing to turn up to two scheduled outings, Sam eventually arrived on her doorstep with tickets to the movies. They had a coffee beforehand and he proposed. Bewildered, Yaffa refused, as she didn't know this smitten soldier. But they were married by the rabbi from Morocco in 1977.

The couple lived in Kiryat Eleazer, a suburb near the family home, and had three children: Shila, Moran and Benel Chaviv. When Sam completed his army service, he became a chef on a ship. For five years the family lived on a cargo ship that travelled to Africa, Europe and even Australia. Sam always dreamed of settling in Australia as he yearned for a quiet country, saying 'Australia is the heaven of the world'. He was the youngest and best chef, and all the captains wanted his high-class cooking, especially his Moroccan doughnuts, known as svenge. As a chef, Sam was easygoing and economical, and his tasty food ensured there was harmony among the sailors. At first, Yaffa educated her children on board the ship with creative craft activities but when Shila started school, Yaffa longed for a stable routine and returned to Haifa while Sam continued to sail.

In 1983, Sam settled in Sydney and started working for a wealthy German restaurateur. He worked long shifts for four dollars an hour in the hope that his boss would sponsor him as a migrant. In 1986, Yaffa arrived in Parramatta with their children but was horrified by Sam's filthy living conditions and missed the support of a Jewish community. One day, Yaffa was travelling by train to Bondi when she saw a truck with a mobile sukkah. Overwhelmed and relieved that she could pray, she started weeping in front of a Yeshivah boy who gave her a biscuit and the rabbi's number. The family decided to make their home in the beachside suburb, where the children attended Yeshivah school.

One day at the Koach Club, a Jewish social club, someone hugged her from behind. He was Marcel's first cousin, David, who recognised Yaffa's strong resemblance to her mother and was moved to tears. The next week, they went to David's home for the Sabbath meal with his ten children. Another guest arrived from the synagogue: he was the kind boy who had offered her a biscuit in the sukkah. Remarkably, he was David's son, Michael, who became the rabbi of the Iraqi community in Sydney.

Yaffa and Sam started baking a dish known as el-maginah – savoury Moroccan potato cakes – which they served to the family's guests. Soon, they received numerous orders from cafes, which the couple managed to fill despite their rudimentary home-kitchen facilities. In the mid-1980s, they opened Sammy's Gourmet Grill in Bondi serving dips, gourmet take-away and fresh juices with yoghurt and honey. Mothers would wait outside with their prams for their healthy drinks. The family decided to move to Melbourne when Sam became the chef at the fashionable Southern Cross Hotel in Bourke Street.

Nowadays, Yaffa cooks her precious family recipes from memory, using whatever ingredients are available. She grows her own herbs – oregano, basil, mint, rosemary, tarragon and sage – to introduce complex flavours to various combinations of spices. On the last day of Passover, in the evening, Yaffa celebrates Mimonah – a Moroccan party during which her house is open for an elaborate celebration. As word gets around, many guests arrive for a feast of cakes, sweets and mufletah (a special bread made from honey and butter). In all, over five hundred friends, neighbours and family attend this celebration, where wine flows and the beat of wild drumming continues throughout the night. It's a Moroccan tradition that Yaffa has preserved in Australia to bestow 'luck and success' upon her guests.

Middle East, Israel

Cooked Salad

Madbucha

In Hebrew dips are known as 'salads'.

2 kg (4 lb) tomatoes

4 red capsicums

100 ml (3½ fl oz) olive oil

2 green chillies, deseeded and chopped

7 cloves garlic, minced

1 tablespoon salt

Cut a tiny cross on the bottom of each tomato and submerge in boiling water for a couple of minutes. The skin should peel from the flesh easily. Once skinned, deseed and roughly chop the tomatoes.

Blister the skin of the capsicums under the grill or by holding with a pair of tongs over a high flame. When blackened, place the capsicums in a plastic bag and seal. After about 10 minutes remove them from the bag. The skin should peel from the flesh easily. (Instead of skinning capsicums, you can simply fry them in olive oil until softened.)

Fry the capsicums and tomatoes in 2 tablespoons of oil in a deep saucepan. Add the chillies and garlic. Cook on a low heat for 2–3 hours, until the mixture thickens into a dip, stirring continuously. Add remaining olive oil and salt. Serve at room temperature.

Serves 8–10

Eggplant Salad with Mayonnaise

Baba Ghanoush

Eggplant is Yaffa's favourite vegetable due to its meaty texture and versatility.
Tahini (sesame seed paste) may be substituted for mayonnaise.

5 eggplants, stems removed

2–3 cloves garlic, minced

1 tablespoon lemon juice

salt

ground white pepper

3–4 tablespoons mayonnaise

Preheat the grill or oven to 200°C (400°F). Roast the eggplants for 30–40 minutes, turning continuously until softened. Alternatively, you can barbecue them.

When cool, skin the eggplants and strain the flesh in a colander to remove any excess water. In a bowl, mash the eggplant and add garlic, lemon juice, salt and pepper to taste, and mayonnaise. Mix. Serve at room temperature.

Serves 8–10

Stuffed Artichokes

Breadcrumbs may be replaced with matzo meal to make this dish suitable for Passover.

12 artichokes

juice of 1 lemon

FILLING

4 tablespoons olive oil

2 onions, finely chopped

500 g (1 lb) minced lamb

500 g (1 lb) minced beef

2 cloves garlic, minced

$\frac{1}{4}$ teaspoon ground white pepper

1 tablespoon chicken stock powder

$\frac{1}{2}$ teaspoon five spice powder

$\frac{1}{4}$ teaspoon ground cinnamon

pinch of dried chilli

2 tablespoons roasted pine nuts

$\frac{1}{4}$ cup flat-leaf parsley, finely chopped

2 tablespoons breadcrumbs or matzo meal

SAUCE

2 tablespoons olive oil

2 onions, finely sliced

$\frac{1}{4}$ teaspoon saffron powder or 6 threads of saffron

2 cups water

4 cloves garlic

$\frac{1}{2}$ bunch parsley, chopped

2 tablespoons chicken stock powder

$\frac{1}{4}$ teaspoon salt

$\frac{1}{4}$ teaspoon ground black pepper

squeeze of lemon juice

Peel each artichoke until only the heart remains. Clean the surrounding fibres with a knife and cut the top off the heart. Once prepared, place the artichokes in lemon juice and water to cover, otherwise they will turn black. Gloves can be used to avoid discolouration of hands.

To make the filling, heat 2 tablespoons of olive oil in a deep frying pan and sauté the onions until soft and golden. Mix the onion with all the filling ingredients except the breadcrumbs.

Drain the artichokes in a colander, spoon the filling into the centre of each heart, and then roll in breadcrumbs, ensuring the edges are coated. Heat 2 tablespoons of olive oil in a deep frying pan and fry the crumbed artichokes on a low heat until they are golden brown.

To make the sauce, heat the olive oil in a saucepan and sauté the onions until browned. If using saffron threads, soak them in $\frac{1}{4}$ cup of hot water until the water changes colour. Add the saffron, water, garlic, parsley, stock, salt and pepper to the onions and bring to the boil.

Place the artichokes in the saucepan with the sauce. Cook on a high heat for 10 minutes and then for 45 minutes on a low heat. Add the lemon juice 5 minutes before serving. Serve with rice or couscous.

Serves 12

Eggplant Salad with Red Capsicums

This is Sam's favourite salad. His mother used to make it for him in Israel.

2 red capsicums

5 eggplants, stems removed

3–4 tablespoons olive oil

$\frac{1}{2}$ teaspoon ground cumin

3 cloves garlic, minced

$\frac{1}{2}$ teaspoon sweet paprika

pinch of dried chilli

$\frac{1}{4}$ teaspoon ground black pepper

juice of 2 lemons

2 tablespoons flat-leaf parsley, finely chopped

Skin the capsicums as in Madbucha (page 69) and slice into thin strips.

Cook, skin and mash the eggplants as in Baba Ghanoush (page 69). Place all the ingredients in a bowl and mix. Serve at room temperature.

Serves 8

Roasted Vegetable Salad

This dish is not a dip, as Israeli 'salads' usually are, but a fresh mix of fragrant ingredients.

2 cobs of corn, husks removed

$\frac{1}{4}$ grey pumpkin, roasted with skin on

2 red capsicums

3 zucchini

2 carrots

6 marinated artichokes, quartered

6 cherry tomatoes, halved

2 cups mesclun salad mix

100 g ($3\frac{1}{2}$ oz) cashews

2 tablespoons sugar

DRESSING

$\frac{1}{4}$ cup chopped dill

2 cloves garlic, minced

$\frac{1}{2}$ teaspoon salt

$\frac{1}{4}$ teaspoon ground black pepper

1 tablespoon mustard

$\frac{1}{4}$ teaspoon honey

3 tablespoons mayonnaise

juice of 1 lemon

$\frac{1}{2}$ teaspoon balsamic vinegar

Preheat the grill to 200°C (400°F). Grill the corn until slightly blackened and chop into rounds about 1 cm ($\frac{1}{2}$ in) thick. Cut the pumpkin, with the skin intact, into thin pieces about 5 cm (2 in) long.

Skin the capsicums as in Madbucha (page 69) and slice into thin strips. Peel the zucchini into long, thin strips with a vegetable peeler and grill or roast until softened. Peel the carrots lengthwise into long, thin strips with a vegetable peeler. Toss all the vegetables with the mesclun salad mix in a large bowl.

Heat the cashews and sugar in a frying pan and stir until the sugar melts and the nuts are coated. Crush the nuts and set aside.

Mix all the dressing ingredients, pour over the salad and toss. Garnish with nuts and serve.

Serves 10

Lamb Casserole with Prunes

Combining meat with dried fruit is typically Middle Eastern.

1.5 kg (3 lb) lamb forequarter chops

SAUCE

6 onions, finely sliced

2 tablespoons olive oil

6 saffron threads

½ cup red wine

1 cup water

20 prunes

3 tablespoons raisins

½ teaspoon ground cinnamon

¼ teaspoon ground mace

2 tablespoons chicken stock powder

pinch of salt

¼ teaspoon ground black pepper

Preheat the oven to 250°C (500°F).

Heat a non-stick frying pan and seal the lamb chops on both sides, so that they retain their shape during cooking.

To make the sauce, heat the oil in a frying pan and sauté the onions until browned. Soak the saffron threads in ¼ cup of hot water until the water changes colour. Combine the onions and saffron in a deep saucepan with remaining sauce ingredients. Bring to the boil.

Line a baking tray with half the sauce. Add the meat and then cover with remaining sauce.

Cover tray with foil, and cook in the oven for 1 hour. Lower temperature to 180°C (350°F) and cook for another hour. Serve hot with couscous.

Serves 6–8

Moroccan Fish Balls

1 kg (2 lb) minced fish (Murray perch, sea perch or flathead)

1 onion, finely chopped

1/2 bunch coriander, finely chopped

1/2 bunch parsley, finely chopped

5 cloves garlic, minced

1 tablespoon ground cumin

pinch of dried chilli

1 tablespoon chicken stock powder

salt

ground black pepper

SAUCE

2 tablespoons olive oil

2 red capsicums, finely chopped

10–12 cloves garlic

60 g (2 oz) sweet paprika

2 cups water

500 g (1 lb) broad beans (frozen)

1/2 bunch coriander, finely chopped

2 carrots, finely chopped

1 tablespoon chicken stock powder

1/4 teaspoon salt

pinch of dried chilli

Mix the fish with the onion, herbs, garlic, spices, stock, salt and pepper in a bowl. Roll mixture into balls and set aside in a baking dish.

To make the sauce, heat the olive oil in a deep saucepan and fry the capsicums until soft. Add the garlic and paprika and fry for a few seconds, stirring continuously. Quickly add water to the saucepan to avoid paprika turning bitter. Add the broad beans and remaining sauce ingredients, except for a handful of the coriander. Cook for 10 minutes, until the sauce is boiling.

Pour the sauce over the fish balls and sprinkle with the remaining coriander. Cover the baking dish and cook on a high heat for 15 minutes. Lower heat and simmer for an hour. Serve hot.

Makes 10

Opposite (front to back) Moroccan Fish Balls and Roasted Vegetable Salad

Hazelnut Meringue Chocolate Mousse Cake

As this cake contains no flour, it is ideal for Passover. To make this dessert parve, cream may be substituted with non-dairy cream, and milk with soy milk or apple juice.

MERINGUE

6 egg whites

2 cups sugar

300 g (11oz) roasted hazelnuts

500 ml (16 fl oz) cream

80 g (3 oz) packet instant vanilla pudding

1 cup milk or soy milk or apple juice

MOUSSE

4 eggs, separated

¾ cup sugar

300 g (11 oz) dark chocolate

2 tablespoons instant coffee

3 tablespoons cocoa

⅓ cup water

½ cup cognac

grated chocolate and crushed hazelnuts for decorating

Preheat the oven to 120°C (240°F). Line two baking trays with baking paper.

To make the meringue, beat the egg whites until they form stiff peaks and then gradually add sugar until well combined. Then load the whites into a piping bag. Pipe small rosettes onto the baking trays and bake for 3 hours. Allow to cool.

Skin the hazelnuts and coarsely chop them. Beat cream, vanilla pudding and milk until thick. Crush the meringues and add them to the cream mixture with the hazelnuts. Pour the mixture into a 28 cm (11 in) springform cake tin and freeze for a few hours or overnight.

To make the mousse, beat the whites until they form stiff peaks, and then gradually add sugar until well combined. Melt the chocolate in a double boiler or in a small saucepan placed in a larger saucepan of boiling water.

Mix the coffee, cocoa, water and cognac, then pour into the chocolate, mixing well. Add the egg yolks, stirring continuously and fold in the egg whites. Pour the mousse over the meringue mixture in the cake tin. Cover with plastic wrap and freeze overnight.

Decorate with grated chocolate and crushed hazelnuts and serve frozen, or defrost and serve cold.

Serves 14–16

Raquella Birner LEBANON

Middle East

I grew up eating Lebanese food. My grandmother was a brilliant cook. Food links me to my family and my heritage. I cook with my head, mixing and tasting. Luckily my friends like Lebanese food. That's how it is.

RAQUELLA was born in Beirut in 1949. Her mother, Esther, is from Lebanon while her father, Maurice, was born on the Greek island of Rhodes. Her father spoke seven languages, including Ladino – a fusion of Spanish and Hebrew – and, Raquella recalls, 'looked like a king'. Fleeing German hostility, Maurice grew up in Marmaris, Turkey, and migrated to Lebanon in the late 1930s. Originally, his family left Spain in 1492 to escape the Inquisition. Raquella's father was an importer of food products, while her mother was a talented dressmaker with more than ten employees, making copies of fashionable haute couture garments. Family life was blissfully chaotic as Esther was one of twelve children.

Raquella herself has three sisters and two brothers. While her family had an apartment in Athens and a house in Tel Aviv, she went to a private French school in Lebanon. She reminisces about the food her grandmother prepared for the Jewish holy days – stuffed intestines and the head of a lamb. As a young girl, she eagerly awaited these special occasions and adored staying at her Nona's. Her grandmother was a talented cook who pickled her own cucumbers, olives and other vegetables.

Lebanese cuisine is labour intensive and time-consuming. A meal starts with mezze platters that include salads, especially tabbouleh and eggplant salad. Like hors d'oeuvres, mezze can also comprise nuts, dips and shashlicks accompanied by arak – an alcoholic drink made from aniseed. Sometimes more than thirty dishes are presented as family and friends enjoy conversation before the main meal. 'Eating from this collection of appetisers is one of my favourite pastimes,' says Raquella. 'There is always a sense of occasion as you dip into the dishes with Arabic bread – sharing, comparing flavours, and allowing the conversation to roam where it will.' Lebanese bread is an essential ingredient of this rich cuisine. There are two types of bread: the flat pita pocket found everywhere in the Middle East, and marook – a thin bread baked on a domed dish over a fire.

Lebanese cuisine uses a lot of lemon and olive oil as well as garlic, spices (nutmeg, cumin, cinnamon, coriander and sumac) and nuts. The staple herbs are parsley and mint. The main course usually consists of meat (lamb is a favourite), chicken or fish, a cooked vegetable, a grain dish and a salad. At the completion of the main course, fresh and dried fruits are served with Turkish coffee, sometimes accompanied by sweet pastries.

At a time when Lebanese Christians, Muslims, Jews and Druze lived together in harmony, Raquella's family often spent their summer holidays in mountain resort towns such as Allay and Hamdoun. As a result, her cooking style shows different regional influences. Healthy ingredients combined with

welcoming hospitality ensure that Raquella's Lebanese home is abundant with variety. Family recipes have been passed down and Raquella relishes spending hours cooking elaborate meals for friends, often preparing snapper or flathead with tahini and hummus or simply served with a fresh salad.

As for many children of Jewish families, Raquella's journey of migration occurred in stages, with her Zionist father initially taking her sisters to Israel after the Six Day War and her aunts and uncles following afterwards. Raquella left Lebanon, alone, at the age of eighteen to travel to Istanbul where her papers were prepared for migration to Israel.

While in Israel for three years, Raquella attended the University of Tel Aviv, completing a Bachelor of Science. There, she met an Australian student, Henry Birner, who was holidaying in Israel, and their romance blossomed. The couple decided to travel to Europe where Henry proposed marriage in a romantic setting in Paris. Raquella's migration to Australia and wedding were delayed due to the Yom Kippur War but she eventually arrived in Melbourne in 1973 and the couple were married soon afterwards. Raquella worked in the genetics department of a hospital before starting a Masters degree, while Henry joined his father in real estate. As she was finishing her studies, they welcomed their son, Daniel.

Even though Raquella's family is dispersed in France, the United States and Israel – she has thirty-six first cousins – they maintain close ties. Raquella often contacts her mother or one of her aunts for advice: 'There is always someone to ring for a recipe.' Nowadays, she enjoys cooking Lebanese banquets for family and friends, rejoicing with the Lebanese refrain *Suhtain – bon appétit*!

Tabbouleh

¼ cup burghul

2 cups finely chopped parsley

½ cup finely chopped mint leaves
(optional)

1 white onion, finely chopped

500 g (1 lb) tomatoes, finely chopped

½ cup lemon juice

1½ teaspoons salt

½ teaspoon ground black pepper

½ cup olive oil

Rinse the burghul, strain in a colander and then squeeze out excess water. Put it in a large mixing bowl and add the parsley, mint, onion, tomatoes and lemon juice. Toss and season. Just before serving add the olive oil. Serve tabbouleh with crisp cos lettuce leaves.

Serves 6–8

Chickpeas with Sesame Seed Paste

Hummus Bi Tahini

A typical Lebanese meal starts with the mezze. This dip is a mainstay at any Middle-Eastern table.

1½ cups chickpeas, soaked overnight

1 teaspoon salt

¾ cup tahini

½ cup lemon juice, or more to taste

2 cloves garlic, minced

½ teaspoon salt

½ teaspoon ground cumin (optional)

pinch of cayenne pepper

2 tablespoons finely chopped parsley

½ teaspoon sumac

1 tablespoon olive oil

Strain the chickpeas and place in a saucepan with three times their volume in water. Add salt, bring to the boil and then simmer until the chickpeas are very soft, about 45 minutes. Drain the liquid, reserving ½ cup of whole chickpeas for the garnish. Purée the remaining chickpeas in a blender. Slowly add the tahini and lemon juice, alternately. Add the garlic, salt, cumin and cayenne pepper. The dip should be thick and smooth but if it seems too thick, thin it with a little water. Pour it onto a serving platter and garnish with reserved chickpeas, sumac and parsley. Drizzle olive oil over the dip.

Serves 8

Raquella Birner

Stuffed Vine Leaves

Mishi Warak Enab

Like the Greek dolmade, these vine leaves are traditionally served as an appetiser.

250 g (9 oz) grape vine leaves

2 potatoes, peeled

½ cup olive oil

3 cups water

½ cup lemon juice

FILLING

1 onion, finely chopped

1 teaspoon salt

¼ cup cooked short-grain rice

1 tablespoon finely chopped mint

300 g (11 oz) tomatoes, finely chopped

2 cups finely chopped parsley

¼ cup lemon juice

½ cup olive oil

1 teaspoon salt

pinch of allspice

pinch of ground cinnamon

pinch of ground white pepper

To make the filling, rub the onion with salt, then mix with the rice, mint, tomatoes and parsley. Stir in the lemon juice, olive oil, salt and spices.

Snip the stems off the vine leaves and rinse in cold water. (If fresh, blanch in boiling water for 2 minutes in three or four lots.) Place a vine leaf, shiny side down, on your work surface. Place 1 tablespoon of filling near the stem end, fold the end and sides over it and roll up firmly to form a cylinder. Repeat the process with remaining leaves.

Slice the potatoes into rounds about 1 cm (½ in) thick. Pour the oil into a heavy-based saucepan and line the base with potato rounds. Above them, pack the vine leaf rolls closely in layers and invert a heavy plate on top to keep rolls in shape during cooking. Add the water and lemon juice, cover and bring to the boil over a moderate heat. Reduce the heat and simmer for 30 minutes, until tender. Serve cold.

Makes 40

Eggplant Salad

Batinjan Mlabbal

1 large eggplant

⅓ cup lemon juice

1 teaspoon white vinegar

1 clove garlic, minced

1 teaspoon salt

pinch of ground black pepper

½ cup finely chopped tomato

2 teaspoons finely chopped parsley

olive oil

Using a pair of tongs, cook the eggplant over the flame of a gas stove on a high heat, turning frequently until it has softened and the skin has blackened. This will give a slightly smoky taste. (Alternatively, roast the eggplant in a hot oven, but the flavour will differ.) Cool and then peel off the skin. Mash the eggplant flesh with a fork and slowly add lemon juice and vinegar. When the mixture is consistent, add the garlic, salt and pepper.

Serve the eggplant garnished with tomato and parsley. Drizzle with olive oil and serve at room temperature.

Serves 4

Raquella Bisner

Opposite Lebanese mezze, including Hummus Bi-Tahini (left)

Lentil and Rice Pilaf

Mjadrah

1 cup brown lentils

4 cups water

½ cup olive oil

2 large onions, finely sliced in semicircles

½ cup rice, washed and strained

1½ teaspoons salt

½ teaspoon ground black pepper

Rinse the lentils and place them in a saucepan with water. Boil for 20 minutes on a medium heat.

Heat the oil in a deep frying pan and sauté the onions until golden brown. Remove half the onion and place on paper towels to drain and remain crisp, to use as a garnish.

Add the rice to the lentils and cook for 10 minutes. Mix in the onion and oil from the frying pan and simmer, uncovered, for about 15 minutes, stirring occasionally to prevent sticking. Season and pour onto a serving platter. Garnish with the remaining onion.

Serves 6

Fish in Tahini Sauce

Samak Bi-Taratur

The tangy tahini perfectly complements the fish in this recipe.
The sauce can be made a day in advance.

2 tablespoons olive oil

1½ cups finely chopped onion

1 kg (2 lb) snapper, blue eye or salmon, fins and scales removed

salt

olive oil

lemon slices and parsley to garnish

SAUCE

½ cup tahini

¾ cup water

½ cup lemon juice

2 cloves garlic, minced

1¼ teaspoons salt

½ cup finely chopped parsley

Heat the oil in a frying pan and sauté the onion. Set aside.

Clean and salt the fish. Refrigerate for several hours and then allow the fish to return to room temperature.

Preheat the oven to 180°C (350°F). Thoroughly rub the outside of the fish with olive oil and bake for 30 minutes, until the flesh seems to flake apart easily with a fork.

To make the sauce, mix the tahini with water and then lemon juice in a blender, adding more lemon juice to taste if necessary. Once the sauce is creamy, add garlic, salt and parsley.

To serve the fish, garnish with lemon slices and parsley and serve the sauce separately. Alternatively, pour the sauce over the baked fish and garnish, or add the onion to the sauce, pour over the fish, return to the oven for a further 20 minutes and serve hot.

Serves 6

Asia
India, Indonesia, Japan, Uzbekistan, Vietnam

Sesame, peanut and coconut oils are typical fats used in Asian recipes, which just happen to suit the Jewish dietary requirements of Kashrut, in which the mixing of milk products with meat products is forbidden. Asian cuisines are also marked by diverse presentation, from the elegant symbolism of Japanese dishes to the fresh simplicity of Vietnamese cuisine. Indian and Indonesian curries, with their intense blend of spices, are marked by fragrant aromas and vivid colours that contrast with the healthy broths of Vietnam. With its reputation for good eating and immense hospitality, the unique Bukharan cuisine of Uzbekistan inventively uses a bag for preparing cholent.

Hannah Elijah INDIA

Asia

I like to share cooking and share recipes. *In Bombay, I used to help my stepmother, Sophie, whose cooking was so wonderful that you couldn't put your spoon down. I recall her making a special halva for Jewish New Year that was stirred for three hours.*

BORN in Bombay in 1924, Hannah traces her ancestors back through ten generations. In the seventeenth century, a member of her family was a standard bearer for Chatrapati Shivaji, a prominent local chieftain who resisted the Moghul incursion into western India. Growing up with two sisters and a brother in a large, close-knit Jewish community, Hannah recalls the painful loss in 1930 of her two sisters from typhoid within three days of each other. Miraculously, Hannah survived the illness. Around the same time, her mother fell from her bed and suffered a stroke. She never recovered.

In 1935, Hannah's father remarried and the house was soon bustling with eight children. Her stepmother, Sophie, was a wonderful cook who lovingly prepared tasty, colourful and spicy Bene-Israel cuisine for her growing family. A swift cook, she often used saffron and chilli for their iridescent colour, combined with coconut and other fresh ingredients.

In 1948, Hannah entered into an arranged marriage with Percy Elijah in Poona and together they lived in the Bombay suburb of Byculla with Percy's brother and his wife. Percy still remembers the first time he saw Hannah – she stood with her father at a local wedding. Percy went to work for Hannah's father as an apprentice in a textile mill. Hannah's father received a medal – the 'Kaiser-I-Hind' – from King George V for his work with the poor. Percy studied science and engineering, eventually working in military engineering services. Speaking the local language, Marathi, Hannah and Percy continued their Indian–Jewish heritage with their own family, living near the local synagogue and observing a Jewish lifestyle. Certain prayers that are particular to Hannah's community are recited for any auspicious occasion, inviting the Prophet Elijah to invoke his blessing.

Percy's Aunt Segulla guided Hannah to cook Indian dishes, including the 'best pilaus'. The women worked together, keeping each other company while they prepared hot meals throughout the day. A small notebook contains all the recipes that Hannah transcribed from her aunt's precious dishes. For the Sabbath, they prepared meat, coconut rice and vegetables. Wine was made from dark grapes and a chapatti-like bread was served for the meal on Friday evening. Although dessert is not a significant aspect of Indian cuisine, fruit and custard were often prepared as well as coconut toffee. Halva was eaten on Rosh Hashanah.

In India all of Hannah's cooking pots were tinned copper and she cooked over a hot coal fire. Later, she used a gas stove at her aunt's house. Dried spices were fried in clay dishes to capture the richest aroma, and tamarind juice was available from the fruit of a tamarind tree in Hannah's garden.

Hannah misses her grinding stone, used to combine the finest of ingredients for her spicy food. For her, the modern blender doesn't produce the same result. Colour and aroma are central to Indian cooking, red, in particular, which is usually accompanied by a pungent fragrance. Chilli, coconut, ginger, garlic, coriander and cardamom are common ingredients along with tamarind and saffron. Desiccated coconut is frequently used and fresh coconut milk accompanies meat curries. Vegetables are often prepared with curry leaves and cumin and mustard seeds to temper these blended flavours.

In India, three hot meals were prepared every day, with domestic helpers grinding spices as well as washing pots and pans. Breakfast consisted of crushed chapatti with milk and sugar, similar to our contemporary cereal. It was difficult to obtain kosher meat, so Hannah arranged for the Muslim butcher to deliver meat to their home. According to Hannah, all religions lived harmoniously in Bombay.

In the 1970s, Hannah completed a catering course in Bombay. She still has the curriculum books from the classes that she attended a couple of times a week, right near her home. She soon found herself busy cooking for her five children.

In 1982, Hannah moved to Australia after a protracted migration process. She was fascinated by Australia, having learned its history along with that of the British Empire while attending the Bombay Scottish High School. After living in a small home in India, she longed for a larger house for her four sons and one daughter. Initially, Hannah arrived with her daughter and oldest son to meet her third son who had already migrated and subsequently sponsored the remaining members of the family. Percy's younger brother was also living in Sydney and gradually the family was reunited.

Hannah and her family are founding members of Melbourne's Sephardi synagogue. Now, she continues to search for fresh ingredients for her exquisite cooking: 'I like to share cooking and share recipes. What's the point in keeping it? You can't cook from your grave!'

Indian Bread

Chapatti

Indians eat chapatti early in the morning. Children eat them crushed with sugar and milk as a cereal. They can also be served with the main meal.

500 g (1 lb) plain flour

1 teaspoon salt

plain flour for dusting

vegetable oil

water

Sieve the flour and salt into a bowl. Make a well in the centre and pour a little water into the well. Mix until dough binds. Dust a bench top with flour and knead the dough. Set it aside to rest for 15 minutes and then knead again. Form the dough into small balls about the size of a golf ball. Smear the dough with oil. Additional flour may be required if the dough is still sticky. Roll them until they are the right consistency. Flatten the dough balls into rounds about 1 cm (½ in) thick.

Fry the rounds on a tava (an Indian hotplate) or non-stick frying pan until cooked, turning them until they puff up. Serve hot or cold.
Makes about 20

Cucumber, Tomato and Onion Salad

2 large tomatoes, finely chopped

2 cucumbers, peeled and finely chopped

1 onion, finely chopped

4–5 stalks coriander, finely chopped

1 tablespoon lemon or lime juice

1 teaspoon sugar

salt to taste

Combine all the ingredients. Refrigerate and serve.
Serves 4

Sweet and Sour Chickpeas

This is an Indian version of cholent.

1¹⁄₂ cups chickpeas

3 cups water

pinch of bicarbonate of soda

1 onion

1–2 green chillies, deseeded

1 teaspoon ground turmeric

2 cloves garlic

1 tablespoon tamarind juice

2 teaspoons soft brown sugar or
the Indian equivalent, jaggery

2 tomatoes

2 tablespoons vegetable oil or ghee

salt to taste

¹⁄₂ teaspoon ground cumin

1 teaspoon garam masala

¹⁄₄ bunch coriander leaves to garnish

Wash and soak the chickpeas in water with bicarbonate of soda overnight.

Boil the chickpeas on a medium heat until cooked, about 20 minutes. Drain and reserve the liquid. In a food processor, blend the onion, chillies, turmeric and garlic to form a paste. In a separate bowl mix the tamarind juice and brown sugar.

Skin the tomatoes by cutting a small cross on the bottom of each tomato and submerging in boiling water for a couple of minutes. The skin should peel from the flesh easily. Finely chop the tomatoes.

Heat the oil in a deep frying pan and fry the paste for a few minutes until fragrant. Add the tomatoes, salt, cumin, garam masala and chickpeas, and cook for 15 minutes. Add the reserved chickpea water if needed.

When cooked, remove from the stove and garnish with coriander leaves. Drizzle with tamarind juice and serve at room temperature.

Serves 6–8

Pea Pilau

Rice is an accompaniment to most main meals. Other vegetables can be substituted for peas.

1¹⁄₂ cups basmati rice

1¹⁄₂ tablespoons olive oil

¹⁄₂ teaspoon cumin seeds

1 onion, finely chopped

10 cloves

7–8 black peppercorns

5 cardamom pods, bruised

1¹⁄₂ cups shelled green peas

¹⁄₂ teaspoon ground turmeric

3 cups hot water

salt to taste

Wash the rice 3–4 times and then spread on a paper towel to absorb the moisture.

Heat the oil in a large saucepan and add cumin seeds. When they splatter, add the onion, cloves, peppercorns and cardamom pods and fry until the onion is pale brown, about 3–4 minutes. Add the rice, peas and turmeric and fry until thoroughly combined. Add water and bring to the boil. Reduce the heat to low, cover and simmer gently for 15 minutes. Uncover and check if the rice is cooked. Additional cooking may be required. Season and, when ready, gently fluff the rice with a fork.

Serves 6–8

Opposite (front to back) Red Chicken Curry, Chapatti and Pea Pilau

Coconut Rice

3 cups water

1 cup coconut milk

1 teaspoon salt

2 cups basmati rice, washed

Bring the water, coconut milk and salt to the boil. Add the rice and simmer for 20 minutes on a low heat, until the water is absorbed and the rice soft.

Serves 8–10

Fish Patties

In India, fresh fish is used to make these fragrant appetisers.
In Australia, canned fish is generally substituted.

1 x 425 g can tuna in spring water

1 onion, finely chopped

3 cloves garlic, minced

2.5 cm (1 in) piece ginger, finely chopped

2 green chillies, finely chopped

¼ bunch coriander leaves, finely chopped

2 slices white bread

2 tablespoons lime or lemon juice

2 eggs, beaten

vegetable oil for frying

Drain the tuna, reserving the liquid. In a large bowl, combine the tuna, onion, garlic, ginger, green chilli and coriander, and mix well. Soak the bread slices one at a time in the reserved liquid. Squeeze the bread and crumble into tuna mixture. Add lime juice and eggs, and mix well. Set aside for 15 minutes. Form into patties, the size of golf balls.

Heat oil in a frying pan and shallow-fry a few patties at a time, turning them over when browned. This will take a few minutes for each side. Drain the patties on paper towels. Serve hot or cold with tomato sauce.

Makes 8–10

Red Chicken Curry

2 large dried red chillies (Kashmiri variety)

6 cm (2½ in) piece ginger, roughly chopped

5 cloves garlic, roughly chopped

2 tablespoons white vinegar

4 tablespoons olive or vegetable oil

4 onions, finely chopped

1 teaspoon salt

1 tablespoon ground coriander

1 teaspoon ground cumin

400 g (14 oz) tomato purée

1.5 kg (3 lb) chicken pieces, skinned and cleaned

Roast the chillies in a saucepan over a low heat for 1–2 minutes. Break them into large pieces, remove the seeds and membrane, and then soak in a little boiling water to soften.

Blend the ginger, garlic, chilli and vinegar in a food processor with a little water until the mixture becomes a smooth paste. Set aside.

Heat the oil in a large saucepan to a medium temperature. Add onions and salt. Stir frequently until the onion turns a pale golden colour. This should take 3–4 minutes. Stir through the coriander and cumin and then add the reserved chilli paste. Stir frequently – do not allow the mixture to burn. Lower the heat and add a little water if it is too dry. Cook until it loses its raw aroma. Add the tomato purée, stir and cook for 2–3 minutes. Add the chicken, stir to incorporate the flavours and then cover. Increase the heat to medium and bring to the boil. Reduce the heat and cook until the chicken is tender, about 20–30 minutes.

Serves 5

Carrot Halwa

Carrot halwa originated from nut dishes introduced to India by traders from the Middle East and Asia Minor during the Moghul period.

4 carrots, grated

2 cups full-cream milk

⅔ cup sugar

3 cardamom pods

2 tablespoons pistachios

4 tablespoons ghee

2 tablespoons sultanas

Combine the carrots, milk, sugar and cardamom pods in a large saucepan and bring to the boil. Lower the heat and cook, stirring occasionally, until all liquid is absorbed, about 1 hour.

Soak the pistachios in hot water, skin and finely chop. In a large frying pan, melt the ghee and then add the cooked carrot mixture, sultanas and pistachios. Fry, stirring continuously, until it changes into a dark orange colour. Serve hot or cold.

Serves 4–6

Bram Khazam INDONESIA

Asia

As a boy, I used to visit two friends over the road from my home in Jakarta. Their mother always invited me to stay for lunch and I couldn't resist the beautiful aroma of her Indonesian cooking. I also have early memories of visiting hawker-style stalls in my neighbourhood, which are part of everyday eating. That's where my love of Indonesian food started.

ORIGINALLY from Iraq, Bram's family was part of the exodus of Jews to the East Indies, in particular, to India and Singapore. The most adventurous went to Java. Bram's mother, Rachel, travelled alone to Indonesia from Basra for her arranged marriage to Ezra, a watchmaker and jeweller, at the age of seventeen.

Born in Jakarta in 1931, Bram delighted in Indonesian food from an early age. He and his four brothers and sister attended a Dutch school, where they learned English and Dutch. Indonesian they learned on the streets. Their friends were both Dutch and Indonesian and, while their upbringing was observant, Bram and his siblings were self-sufficient and independent. Sometimes they would take their pocket money and go away for a day on adventures to hawker stalls and markets, delighting in eating gado gado, sate and rujak – a sour fruit like unripe mango accompanied by a sauce of palm sugar, tamarind, red chilli and salt with an intensely sour and unique flavour.

Bram fondly recalls his childhood home in a middle-class residential street in Jakarta and relishes early memories of mouth-watering flavours. He partly learned to cook delectable Indonesian feasts by observing hawker stalls offering outdoor, casual eating. He ate meat for the first time in the late 1930s when frozen lamb was imported from Australia and promptly fell ill as his mother didn't know how to prepare it. The family predominantly ate fish, chicken and eggs.

In 1941, Bram's contented family life was thrown into disarray when Indonesia fell under Japanese occupation and anyone who wasn't Indonesian was rounded up. His father and older brothers were interned in a camp in Jakarta run by Japanese and Indonesian soldiers. Bram remembers walking past the camp to wave at his father. For a while, Bram stayed at home with his mother, sister and younger brother but soon they too were rounded up and taken to an old jail, Tanah Tinggi, then Tangerang. Eventually, in 1943, Bram was transferred alone to a boy's camp called Grogol, which was a former psychiatric institution. At the age of twelve, he had no contact with his parents for six months.

Opposite Carrot Halwa

Bram was sent to a camp in central Java where he found his beloved brothers and father. In 1945, two significant events unfolded: the Japanese capitulated, breaking their allegiance with Germany, and the atom bomb was dropped on Hiroshima. When the Japanese gave up, Bram jumped the camp's fence with his brother Morris. The pair headed straight to the market to devour hawker food. They were officially released and returned to Jakarta to be reunited with the rest of the family who had, in the meantime, also been released.

Sadly, Bram's paternal grandmother, Hannah, died in Tangerang. Previously, while living with the family in Jakarta, she had taught her daughter-in-law to cook. Bram remembers constantly hearing the stamping of the mortar and pestle as delectable hot dishes were prepared for lunch and dinner. A favourite was when the two women cooked a type of unleavened bread that was set on an inverted wok above a fire.

Bereft, the family set up temporary residence with another Jewish family. Gradually life returned to normal and Saturday lunch became a highlight of the week for the reunited family. Hamin, like cholent, was prepared with a risotto-like consistency. Cooked in advance, it was kept warm by covering the vessel in blankets. At this time, the Khazams began to share their residence with an Indonesian aristocratic family from a high caste. The family had a cook and Bram remembers watching her make beef rendang, which must be cooked thoroughly with a lot of coconut milk and fragrant salam leaves. Explaining her technique as she went, she became an important influence on this curious young boy, who would develop a lifelong passion for Indonesian cuisine.

Bram embarked on medical studies at the University of Jakarta but eventually went with his older brother Max to Amsterdam to further his education. He graduated from university in 1959 and spent two years in the air force doing compulsory military service. Bram prepared Indonesian food far from home, remembering recipes from his childhood. Meanwhile, his mother, father and sister had migrated to Melbourne, as life in Indonesia was becoming perilous and an uncle was able to sponsor their travel. Planning to become a dermatologist, Bram visited his parents in Melbourne before starting specialist training. However, while there, he met his future wife, Gabrielle, and his plans soon changed: the couple were married in 1963. Bram remembers Gabrielle's mother preparing 'the best gefilte fish ever tasted'.

Bram cooks from observation and memory but he has amassed menus over the years by asking Indonesian cooks for their recipes and by collecting Dutch/Indonesian cookbooks – some even dating from the 1920s. Indonesian food is more fragrant than spicy, with colour, especially red and yellow, an essential aspect of the cuisine. Recipes are flexible, allowing for creativity: 'If you ask an Indonesian cook what quantity to prepare, they will respond "just enough"'. One of Bram's main ingredients is a mild chilli paste used not only for flavour but to embellish dishes with a vibrant colour. He also recommends: 'When something is sweet, add a little salt to enrich flavours and create harmony'.

Bram often uses peanut oil in his signature dishes, for its slight aroma. 'Don't be afraid to experiment,' he says. 'I rely on memories to create authentic Indonesian flavours but memory is idealised!' Nowadays, apart from preparing banquets for his family, Bram works as a general practitioner and psychotherapist specialising in treating cancer patients.

Indonesian Salad

Lotek

'There are several varieties of gado gado, an increasingly popular Indonesian salad with peanut sauce. Then there are local varieties of gado gado, such as its Javanese form (Batavia—old Jakarta, Bandung and Surabaya styles) and the Sumatran (Padang) style. Even various suburbs can have their own choice of ingredients and methods of cooking. Lotek is a fresh-tasting hawker-style variety with an uncooked peanut sauce. The traditional ingredients kencur (lesser galangal root) and prawn paste can be safely left out.'

DRESSING

1 tablespoon tamarind juice or juice of 1 lime or lemon

1 small cube palm sugar, dissolved

1 tablespoon mild chilli paste

200 ml (7 fl oz) hot water

1 cup peanuts, fried and ground or 3 heaped tablespoons peanut butter

SALAD

3 tablespoons vegetable oil

250 g tempeh, cubed

300 g tofu, cubed

½ iceberg lettuce

1 head broccoli, steamed

¼ cabbage, steamed

1 cup bean shoots

2 potatoes, steamed

1 Lebanese cucumber, finely sliced

2 hard-boiled eggs, sliced

½ cup fried chopped spring onions or fried crackers

spring onions, fried and chopped to garnish

hot chilli sauce to taste (optional)

To make the dressing, grind the tamarind juice, palm sugar and chilli paste with a mortar and pestle until it forms a paste. Add hot water to dilute it, then add the peanuts and mix to a smooth, thick emulsion, the consistency of cream. Add water as needed.

To make the salad, heat the oil in a frying pan and fry the tempeh and tofu cubes until they are golden brown, then drain them on absorbent paper. Tear the lettuce into bite-size pieces. Cut the broccoli into florets and slice the cabbage. Blanch the bean shoots for a few seconds in boiling water. Cool the cooked vegetables under tap water to avoid wilting, then dry them with paper towels. Cut the potatoes into fine slices.

Arrange the cucumber slices with the other vegetables on a plate. Add the tofu, tempeh, egg and potato. Pour the dressing over the salad and sprinkle the spring onions over the top. Add hot chilli to taste.

Serves 6

Spicy Fish

Sambal Goreng Ikan

This dish (in which 'ikan' means 'fish') can also be made with chicken, tender veal or eggs.
A sambal goreng (spicy fried dish) is usually made medium–hot with chillies (or pepper if preferred).
Serve with white rice.

400 g (14 oz) rockling, cut into thirds
or quartered

3 tablespoons peanut oil

1 large onion, finely chopped

1 bulb lemongrass, crushed, or 3 kaffir
lime or salam leaves

1 tablespoon coriander seeds

1 teaspoon ground turmeric

hot water or fish stock

1 tablespoon tamarind juice
or lemon juice

3–4 tablespoons coconut milk

salt to taste

palm sugar to taste

Marinade

2 tablespoons tamarind juice

$\frac{1}{2}$ tablespoon salt

Basic Paste (Bumbu)

3 cloves garlic

1 cm ($\frac{1}{2}$ in) piece ginger, finely sliced

1 tablespoon chilli paste

$\frac{1}{2}$ tablespoon tomato paste or
1 tablespoon tamarind juice

5 candlenuts

Marinate the fish for 1 hour in the marinade. This will remove any unpleasant fishy smell or taste.

To make the paste, grind the garlic, ginger, chilli paste, tomato paste and candlenuts in a mortar and pestle.

Heat the oil in a saucepan until it shows a slight haze but isn't smoking. Sauté the onion until softened. Reduce the heat to low, add the paste and lemongrass (you can use lemongrass, kaffir lime leaves and salam leaves but use half quantities in this case) while stirring gently, adding a little water to prevent burning. Fry gently until the oil separates out and the fragrance is released.

Dry-fry the coriander seeds and grind to a powder. Mix the coriander and turmeric with a little hot water to make a wet paste and add to the saucepan. Add a little more water to the sauce, but avoid adding too much – keep the sauce thick.

Add the fish, without the marinade, and simmer over a low heat, taking care not to break up the fish. Add the tamarind juice and coconut milk and stir gently. Do not cover the saucepan once the coconut milk has been added. Simmer for 5 minutes, until the fish is cooked. Add salt and palm sugar. The dish is ready when the oil is diminished and the sauce coats the spoon.

Serves 4

Curried Chicken, Javanese Style

This dish is a thick brown–red curry with an appetising appearance due to the separated oil.

80 ml (3 fl oz) peanut oil

1 large onion, finely chopped

1 bulb lemongrass

4–5 dried salam leaves (daon salam), available from Asian shops

4–5 kaffir lime leaves

1 cup hot water or chicken stock

2 skinless chicken breasts, cut into bite-size pieces or 1 chicken, cut into 10 pieces

200 ml (7 fl oz) coconut milk

1 small cube palm sugar

1 tablespoon tamarind juice

hot chilli sauce or ground black pepper to taste

INDONESIAN CURRY POWDER

1 tablespoon coriander seeds

½ tablespoon cumin seeds

½ tablespoon caraway seeds

1 teaspoon ground turmeric

BASIC PASTE

3 cloves garlic

5 candlenuts

½ tablespoon mild chilli paste

1 cm (½ in) thick slice ginger

1 bulb lemongrass, finely chopped

To prepare the curry powder, dry-fry the coriander, cumin and caraway seeds until fragrant. Grind the warm spices in a coffee grinder to a fine powder. Mix with turmeric. Only 1 tablespoon of curry powder will be required for this dish. Store the remaining powder in a container in a cool place.

To make the paste, blend the garlic, candlenuts, chilli paste, ginger and lemongrass.

Heat the oil in a deep frying pan and sauté the onion over a high heat until it yellows and starts to look dry. Lower the heat and add the paste, frying gently until the oil separates out.

Cut the stalk of the lemongrass about 15 cm (6 in) above the bulb and crush with the salam and kaffir lime leaves in a mortar. (These herbs can be used singly or in combination. When using them in combination reduce the quantity of each to half.) Add the lemongrass mixture to the frying pan and then the stock or water, 1 tablespoon at a time, to keep the dish from burning. Increase the heat to medium and add the chicken, coating it with the mixture.

Mix 1 tablespoon of the curry powder with a few tablespoons of water to make a wet paste and add to the frying pan. Continue to fry for half a minute on a low heat. Slowly add ½ cup of water and simmer for a couple of minutes. Pour the coconut milk over the simmering dish, taking care not to let it boil. When using coconut milk, use a plastic or wooden spoon to prevent the coconut from turning dark.

Add the palm sugar and return to a simmer, uncovered, on a low heat until the oil separates out. The sauce should be thick enough to coat the mixing spoon. Remove from heat, add the tamarind juice and hot chilli sauce to taste. Serve with steamed white rice.

Serves 5

Beef Rendang

'This is a Sumatran dish devised as a way of cooking tough buffalo meat by simmering it for hours in spices and coconut milk. At the end of the cooking process, the coconut milk will have released its oil content and begun to fry the tenderised meat pieces to a dark brown colour. The coconut itself has now become crusty and very tasty. That lengthy cooking process can be somewhat reduced by using more tender meat cuts, and the dish should finish as a dry dark curry. It keeps well and can be frozen.'

80 ml (3 fl oz) peanut oil

1 large onion, finely chopped

500 g (1 lb) topside beef

5–6 salam leaves or 2 bulbs lemongrass or 5 kaffir lime leaves

400 ml (14 fl oz) coconut milk

1 cup water or stock

1 tablespoon tamarind juice

palm sugar to taste

hot chilli sauce or ground black pepper to taste

salt to taste

BASIC PASTE (BUMBU)

3 cloves garlic

1 cm (½ in) thick slice ginger

5 candlenuts

1 tablespoon mild chilli paste

CURRY POWDER

1 tablespoon coriander seeds

½ tablespoon ground turmeric

hot water or stock

To make the paste, pound the garlic, ginger, candlenuts and chilli paste using a mortar and pestle or a blender.

Heat the oil in a saucepan and sauté the onion until it yellows and starts to look dry. Reduce the heat to low, add the paste and fry for 1–2 minutes, until the fragrance is released.

Remove the fat and gristle from the beef and cut into large bite-size pieces. Add the pieces to the saucepan, coating them with the sauce.

To make the curry powder, dry-fry the coriander seeds until fragrant and then grind them to a powder. Add the turmeric and mix with a little hot water to make a paste. Add the curry powder, salam leaves and coconut milk to the beef and simmer while stirring gently. Add water and simmer on a low heat until cooked, up to 4 hours.

When the dish is almost dry, add the tamarind juice, palm sugar, hot chilli sauce and salt to taste. Stir continuously to prevent burning. Serve hot.

Serves 4

Yoko Ryan JAPAN

Asia

There are strong similarities between Japanese and Jewish food. They are both festival cuisines: they tell stories through symbolic cooking that we pass down to our children, from one generation to the next.

BORN in the governmental town of Shizuoka in 1949, Yoko grew up near Mount Fuji with two younger sisters, Kozue and Yoshiko. Yoko's father, Gunichi, loved timber and established a lacquer-ware factory at the back of their house. He made exquisite Japanese lacquer and music boxes for export, in particular to the United States. 'I clearly remember the smell of lacquer and the tinkering of jewellery boxes in my home. The artisans worked in the back of our house in a calm and dust-free room.'

Yoko also remembers with fondness the smell of wood from a timber bath next to the kitchen and the cedar serving bowls. 'There was no washing machine or rice cooker when I was a child and we pumped water from a well. Everything was cooked on a charcoal fire.' When Yoko was in high school her mother, Nakako, started cooking lessons and consequently began preparing Western food such as hamburgers and Scotch eggs. Western food was progressively introduced to Japan in the 1950s and 1960s, which was an exciting time for Yoko. Rice, however, remains a staple of most meals in Japan, often served in a lunch box with a pickled plum – umeboshi – and shiso leaves (a Japanese spice).

Yoko attended a strict Irish-Catholic girls' school where her teachers were nuns. But her family practised Buddhism and Shintoism, more as a way of life than a religious belief, which involved visits to the shrine and temple on special occasions. During summer there was a festival, like a fair, with outdoor food stalls, dancing and celebrations. New Year was a special festival and Yoko remembers wearing her kimono and hair decorations. The three-day-long festival began with the striking of a bell in the temple and was celebrated with a bowl of long, soba noodles (toshi koshi soba), symbolising a long life, and special rice cakes (omochi) made by the arduous process of beating rice in a large, timber bowl until it becomes flat and sticky like gum. Dried sardines were enjoyed for a healthy year while shredded white radish and carrots soaked in sweet vinegar were eaten because of their merry colour.

Complementary and medicinal aspects of Japanese cuisine are significant. Radish is served grated on tempura as it is thought to calm the stomach, while ginger is often presented alongside fish to eradicate the latter's strong smell. Yoko savours the variety of ingredients in Japanese cuisine as well as the exquisite and delicate presentation. Even children's lunches are beautifully presented, with animal-shaped vegetables accompanied by rice mountains with flags on top. 'As a child, I used to love going to the family restaurant at Matsuzaka-ya Department Store. I would have oko sama – children's lunch. Japanese cuisine is seasonal so as to ensure varied and fresh ingredients. Spring is a time for

baby shoots while autumn is symbolised by a host of different mushrooms and seafood.'

When Yoko finished school in Shizuoka, she lived in Tokyo for two years to learn English at an American school. Then, she worked as an au pair for the British consul's family at the embassy in Azabu. Keen to continue practising her English, Yoko was introduced by her friend Chieko to Adam Ryan, who was backpacking through South-East Asia and teaching English. The two started meeting in various coffee shops. When Yoko finished her studies, she was supposed to return home and work in her father's business, but instead, with an adventurous and independent spirit, she travelled to New York and met Adam again.

Yoko and Adam decided to marry, and travelled to Melbourne to meet Adam's parents, who are from a traditional Polish Jewish family. (The family name was actually 'Rybjyzan' but Australians found it difficult to pronounce and spell, so Adam shortened the name to 'Ryan' by combining the first two and the last two letters.) Yoko recalls her future father-in-law welcoming her with flowers on their first meeting. Eventually, she summoned the courage to return home and tell her parents about her pending marriage. Traditionally, if there are no sons in a Japanese family, when the oldest daughter marries, her husband changes his name to hers for perpetuity. 'But it didn't work out like that for me.' Instead, she packed her bags with the help of her sisters and, with $100 to her name, set off for a new life in Australia.

When Yoko arrived in Melbourne in 1971, she lived with Adam's family. She started working at the Japanese Consulate and the couple married the next month in a quiet ceremony in a registry office with a few friends. Her mother-in-law would cook chicken soup, croquettes and grilled chops, using a lot of onions and garlic: 'I loved her tasty food. I enjoyed eating T-bone steak and mash every day.' Yoko converted to Judaism ten years after marrying Adam.

In the late 1970s and 1980s, when Yoko started entertaining Adam's business associates, she prepared Japanese food for them. She avidly read Japanese cookbooks, then adapted the dishes for an Australian context. For her, the decorative aspects of her native cuisine are essential to its charm. There is balance and harmony in the food Yoko prepares, as she believes that 'cooking must be artistic'. Even the most simple food is presented with a delicate leaf from her garden so that it not only tastes delicious but also looks appetising. Cooking with intuition and the immense pleasure derived from seeing her guests enjoy her cuisine, Yoko often prepares temaki sushi – home-style sushi – in which all the fresh ingredients are placed on the table for guests to roll in a seaweed cone.

Yoko has skilfully adapted aspects of Japanese cooking to an Australian Jewish lifestyle. When preparing schnitzels, she adds sesame seeds and crumbed seaweed to the breadcrumbs for flavour and colour. Hamburger meat is mixed with tofu so it becomes softer, while macaroni is fried with butter and soy sauce to enhance flavours. For the Sabbath, Yoko prepares both chicken soup with kreplach and lokshen as well as temaki sushi. She loves to cook for her family of four children and for her grandchild. Even though her mother and her sisters still live in Shizuoka, where Nakako is a tea ceremony teacher, Yoko is inextricably linked to her heritage, annually performing the ancient ritual of the tea ceremony in her adopted country.

Above Fish in Ginger Soy Sauce

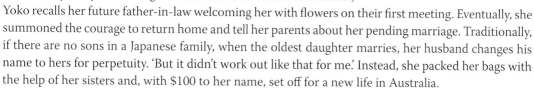

Roll-your-own Sushi

Temaki Sushi

Japanese food is appreciated for its wonderful combinations of flavours and textures as well as its appealing presentation. The presentation of this dish involves the guest as well as the cook. 'Te' means hand, 'maki' means roll. The fish options listed here are all good fish to eat raw. However, be sure to tell the fishmonger that you will be using the fish for sushi so that they can recommend the freshest of the day. You may like to experiment with a little bit of mayonnaise or fish roe. Instead of raw fish, smoked salmon or finely sliced roast chicken or beef can be substituted.

4 boned fish fillets (tuna, salmon, ocean trout, yellow tail or snapper)

3 eggs

1 tablespoon mirin

1 tablespoon water

1–2 packets seaweed

1 avocado, cut into fine slices

1 Lebanese cucumber, deseeded and finely sliced

wasabi paste

SUSHI RICE

2 cups short-grain rice

4 cups water

½ cup white vinegar, slightly warmed

pinch of salt

75 g (2½ oz) sugar

Slice fish with a very sharp knife into 1 cm (½ in) thick pieces and place on a flat dish.

Beat the eggs with mirin and water. Heat a small frying pan, 20 cm (8 in) in diameter, until very hot. Pour in the egg mixture, lower the heat and cook until the omelette is firm. When cool, cut into thick pieces.

To make the sushi rice, combine the rice and water in a saucepan, bring to the boil and simmer on a low heat for 20 minutes, until the water is absorbed and the rice is cooked. Mix the vinegar, salt and sugar and pour over the hot rice. When mixing the rice, use a rice spatula. Try to fan rice while mixing, as this creates a glaze and prevents gooeyness.

To assemble, divide a sheet of seaweed into quarters. Place a small amount of rice onto a piece of seaweed, covering half the area. On top of the rice place a piece of fish or omelette, avocado slice and cucumber slice. Dab a little wasabi onto the rice and then carefully roll the seaweed into a cone. (It should not contain too many ingredients or it will break.)

Temaki sushi is best eaten immediately.

Serves 4

Fish in Ginger Soy Sauce

Ginger is a basic ingredient in Japanese sautéed dishes. It is helpful in counteracting the strong odour of fish.

½ cup water

1 tablespoon sugar

80 ml (3 fl oz) soy sauce

1 tablespoon sake

4 white fish fillets (orange roughy, john dory, flathead or snapper)

10 fine slices ginger, skin on

Mix water, sugar, soy sauce and sake, and bring to the boil. Add fish and ginger and cook for 5 minutes, until fish is cooked. While cooking, keep the fish coated with the sauce.

Serve with green vegetables.

Serves 4

Beef in Teriyaki Sauce

Teriyaki is often used for meat and fish as well as chicken. 'Teri' means shine or glaze, produced by the mirin in the cooking process. 'Yaki' means to grill or sauté.

600 g (1¼ lb) fillet beef

2 tablespoons soy sauce

2 tablespoons mirin

1 tablespoon sake

1 tablespoon sugar

1 tablespoon canola oil

Finely slice the beef (if you freeze the meat first it is easier to slice). Mix the soy sauce, mirin, sake and sugar in a bowl, then pour it over the beef to marinate for at least 1 hour; overnight is preferable.

Heat the oil in a frying pan (no oil is required if using a non-stick frying pan). Drain the marinade from the beef and stir-fry the pieces in batches, ensuring they are sealed on both sides. Serve with finely sliced cabbage.

Serves 4

Ice-cream with Adzuki Beans

*Adzuki beans are small, dark red, oval beans with a strong, sweet and nutty flavour.
Popular in Japanese cuisine, they make a sweet paste.*

500 g (1 lb) adzuki beans
1½–2 cups sugar
vanilla ice-cream

Submerge the beans in water and bring to the boil, covered. Cook until the beans are soft, about 1–1½ hours. Add the sugar and cook for a further 30 minutes, uncovered, stirring continuously until beans form a gooey consistency and water has evaporated.

Serve at room temperature with vanilla ice-cream and/or fruit.
Serves 8–10

Miriam Atzil UZBEKISTAN

Asia

In the old days, all the women cooked together, not in separate houses. Everyone would come over two or three hours early. Mum would bring flour, my grandmother would bring onions – each person a different ingredient. It was a social and community occasion as we would sit at low tables preparing a vast meal for our extended family of one hundred people. I miss this special time. There was little furniture but the door was always open and there was plenty to share.

MIRIAM was born in 1946 in Bukhara, a little town in Uzbekistan, which is part of the former Soviet Union. She grew up in a large, orthodox family of four sisters and two brothers. Her great-great-grandfather was a talented architect from Kabul, Afghanistan, called Menachem Kavuli (from 'Kabul'). In the mid-nineteenth century, he built saunas for wealthy clients while his wife made elaborate floor and wall coverings that would take up to a year to sew.

The Shah was immensely impressed with Menachem's skills as an architect, especially his accurate way of working out the number of bricks required for a building, and he was invited to settle in Bukhara. Menachem relocated on the condition that he could take his brothers as well as close family members, ensuring there would be the minimum number of ten men to create a minyan (or quorum) for Jewish prayers. Menachem built a mosque in Bukhara with an adjoining ritual bathing room but when Lenin came to power all religions were banned. Today, this building is a music and arts school that Miriam and her sisters attended. It is proudly adorned with a plaque reading, 'Menachem Kavuli built this mosque.' There are now seven generations of architects on this side of Miriam's extensive family.

Miriam grew up with her mother, Yaffa, grandmother, Miriam, and great-grandmother, Betty, all of whom are herbalists. She remembers Betty keeping herbs in a dark room in jars that weren't labelled. Remarkably, Betty could identify herbs by sight and smell. When Miriam was eleven years old, a man visited her great-grandmother for a consultation. He brought a basket of freshly baked bread as it was understood that clients would barter goods from their own trade in exchange for the herbs. When Betty asked what he did for a living, he replied 'gravedigging', at which she exclaimed 'I am not ready to die yet!'

Betty married Yakov Meir at the age of twelve, just after her bat mitzvah. They went to Israel for one year by camel and conceived on their return. Betty's second daughter, Miriam, fell in love with wealthy Jacob, whose family went to live abroad. Jacob chose to stay with his beloved Miriam and they

had seven children who became teachers. Eventually, when both Miriam and Betty were widowed, they lived together in a fifteen-metre long room with magnificent carpets on the floor that the family would sit on for sumptuous feasts.

Among the hundred family members who would attend the Sabbath meal on Friday night, everyone had a part in the preparation. The younger generation set the table, while the women would talk, sing and listen to music as they cooked. Often, chicken soup was prepared with potatoes, radish and carrots or hand-made pasta. Then coriander carp – a unique Bukharan dish – was served on large platters. Guests ate with their hands from abundant platters, sharing these delicious dishes.

Miriam's parents met when her father was the principal at the school where Yaffa taught biology and botanical studies. He was smitten the first time he saw his future bride and presented her with a huge bouquet of purple flowers the following summer. From that year, every first of September was commemorated by Yakov giving his wife purple flowers. Sadly, Yakov died when Yaffa was just thirty-two, with seven children. On the day of his funeral, all schools were closed to bid farewell to the renowned teacher. In 1953, young Miriam moved to Namangan with her grandmother and mother. There were approximately 250 Jewish families in Namangan and Miriam remembers celebrating festivals from the Jewish calendar. Sukkot was celebrated in autumn, with the temporary dwelling covered in a canopy of grapes decorated with pomegranates and seasonal fruit.

For Purim, every family languished on their verandas in the summer heat. Her mother would dress as Queen Esther and perform *Megillat Esther*, the story of Purim. The day before, they would prepare hamantashen – triangular biscuits made from sweet dough (literally 'haman pockets') – and special 'Purim samosas' filled with meat. For Passover, dishes were cleansed with ash from the tanur, or clay oven. Unleavened bread – matzo – was prepared for this festival. As Miriam became older, she was trusted with the rolling pin and gently and carefully rolled out the thin dough, a reverence she has always retained. 'All dishes must be beautifully prepared for special occasions.' Cooking was always a co-operative and joyful process.

Miriam learned to cook her precious Bukharan recipes from observation. 'No one taught me recipes. They said, "Watch and steal the idea with your eyes. Don't ask questions." This is how I taught my daughter-in-law to cook. If you see that something has to be done, just do it. If I have to tell you, then the job is partly done.'

Bukharan cuisine is seasonal: quinces are prepared in late autumn while winter warmer chicken is prepared in the colder months. Nutrition is central to Miriam's cooking. Having studied herbal medicine over the past forty years, she now understands the family rituals of not mixing hot and cold food; refraining from drinking tea and fruit straight after a meal to allow for digestion; and other sensible nutritional customs.

Prepared on Friday afternoon, Bukharan cholent cooks overnight, ready for when the men return from synagogue at midday on Saturday. Miriam remembers the beautiful aroma that filled their home. After the meal, they'd play chess and tell stories.

In 1979, Miriam's younger sister, Regina, travelled to Australia, while the family migrated to Israel. Miriam's uncle gave her three utensils to take to Israel: a rolling pin, a wooden chopping board and a mortar and pestle. When Miriam was cooking on ulpan in Beer Sheva, all the neighbours would come to smell her delectable food and lick the cholent bag!

Eventually, members of Miriam's family started to migrate to Australia and Miriam arrived in 1985. Now, she continues her family tradition of exalting the Sabbath meal by sharing the cooking with her extended family and visiting the Sephardi synagogue, Hamerkaz Shelanu, in Melbourne. For her, meals are a form of communication: a way for people to connect and unite. 'I love the preparation and planning of meals. I can imagine the tastes. Spices are important as you don't want to spoil with too much – that's the secret. I prepare with love in my heart because that is what I want to share with others.'

Above Winter Warmer Chicken

Coriander Carp

Found in the local river, carp prepared in the Bukharan way is usually eaten on Friday night.
Coriander is a popular herb in Bukharan cooking and it is combined with plenty of garlic in this recipe.

1 bunch coriander, chopped
500 ml (16 fl oz) water
6 cloves garlic, peeled and crushed
300 ml (11 fl oz) olive oil
1.5 kg (3 lb) carp, cut into cutlets
½ teaspoon salt

Combine coriander, water and garlic in a bowl. Heat the oil in a deep frying pan and fry the cutlets for a few minutes on each side until cooked through. Soak the fried cutlets in the coriander mix for 10 minutes to allow the flavours to be absorbed. Add salt.
Spoon onto a platter and serve hot or cold.
Serves 6–8

Winter Warmer Chicken

This is a warming winter dish for very cold days. It is the Bukharan version of chicken soup.

1 kg (2 lb) chicken
2 tablespoons olive oil
2 onions, chopped
1 carrot, chopped
1 red capsicum, chopped
1 teaspoon salt
½ teaspoon ground cumin
½ teaspoon ground coriander
2 large quinces, quartered

Quarter the chicken and remove the skin. Heat the oil in a saucepan and sauté the onions until slightly brown. Add the carrot and capsicum and fry until softened. Add the chicken, cover and steam for 5 minutes.

Mix the salt, cumin and coriander into the chicken, then add the quince and simmer for 20 minutes, until the quince is softened but still has its shape.

To serve, place the chicken on a platter, cover with quince and pour the sauce over the top.
Serves 6–8

Cholent in a Bag

Oshi Sabo

This unique version of cholent is cooked in a bag and boiled in a stockpot.

500 g (1 lb) brown rice, washed

1 kg (2 lb) lamb leg, finely chopped

1½ onions, finely chopped

200 g (7 oz) sultanas

2 carrots, finely chopped

4 granny smith apples, peeled and finely chopped

¼ teaspoon ground cinnamon

¼ teaspoon ground nutmeg

1 teaspoon salt

50 ml (1½ oz) olive oil

Thoroughly combine all the ingredients in a large bowl. Fill an oven bag with the mixture, ensuring it is tightly packed. Place the oven bag into a muslin or cloth bag. Tie the top of the bag with string and place into a large saucepan filled with water to cover. Bring to the boil and then simmer on low heat for 16 hours, ensuring the water is topped up to cover the bag.

When ready, empty the contents into a large bowl and mix well. Serve hot.

Serves 8–10

Asia, Uzbekistan

Bukharan Delight

Larz

A sweet made with sugar syrup and nuts.

200 g (7 oz) sugar

100 ml (3½ fl oz) water

200 g (7 oz) almonds, finely crushed

50 g (1½ oz) walnuts, finely crushed

½ teaspoon rosewater

30 g (1 oz) plain flour

50 g (1½ oz) pistachios, finely crushed

Heat the sugar and water until a syrup forms. Add the almonds, walnuts and rose water, and mix until thick.

Sprinkle flour on a flat round baking tray about 18 cm (7 in) in diameter. Spread the cooked mixture onto the tray and level with a knife. Sprinkle the pistachios on top and allow to set. While the mixture is setting, cut it into diamonds. Refrigerate. Serve when the mixture has hardened.

Serves 8–10

Miriam Greenfield VIETNAM

I can close my eyes and remember the large
quadrangle of our home in Hanoi at harvest time.
There was a pot in each corner, brimming with cooked
sweet potatoes for the workers who harvested our rice,
which was piled high in the centre of the yard.
Singing and enjoying themselves, everybody
worked together.

BORN in Hanoi in 1944, Miriam grew up in a scholastic household lined with books. Miriam, along with her engineer father, Tran Hoai An, and her mother, Lien, lived with her full extended family, including Lien's three sisters and Miriam's grandparents, in a large house with a quadrangle. Each of the sisters was assigned a particular dish for festive occasions – spring rolls, soup or salads – repeating the recipe until their mother decided that it had been perfected. The women prepared food together, with Miriam now realising that she subconsciously took it all in as she passed by the hectic kitchen, 'eventually carrying the smells of my childhood into adulthood'.

A beautiful city, Hanoi comprises thirty-six streets, each named after a trade. Hang Dao is the fruit street, with luscious peaches, and from the age of five Miriam would walk along it on hot balmy nights with her nanny. At the south gate, they would stop to enjoy cua nam – tiny cups of lemon sorbet. Speaking French and Vietnamese at home, Miriam savoured bread, chicken pâté and omelette as well as typical Vietnamese dishes. Her grandfather, Lap, was fussy about food: his wife was the only one allowed to prepare his meals. 'None of the four daughters was qualified to cook for him.' A lacquer-ware artist interested in scholarly pursuits, Lap would even wake his four daughters at 3 a.m. to have them study with him.

Miriam's upbringing was strict in all ways. 'If I dropped one grain of rice, I would quickly hide my misdemeanour. I was not allowed to pick up my chopsticks until the oldest person had.' Her grandmother cooked three hot meals a day, ensuring that she was in the kitchen all day long. Fresh produce was purchased from the market daily, with special delicacies prepared for Tet, the lunar new year, in January or February. A sticky rice cake with mung beans and meat in the centre was wrapped in banana leaf and held by a piece of string while it boiled in a large barrel over a charcoal fire. The family would gather around the fire and talk all night, until the cake was ready. It was then laid across a long timber stool and pressed with planks of timber to remove excess water before being eaten on New Year's Day.

In 1954, the family fled their house at the outbreak of war. Part of the family escaped to the south and for two troubled years Miriam and her mother lost contact with them during the communist uprising.

'We stayed in army barracks. The city was full of strangers and podiums where landlords were put on trial. Peasants came to the city and took over our house. We lived in fear and hiding.' Robbed of her childhood, Miriam was taken south with her mother by the last US carrier. At the end of the war, Miriam and her mother searched for missing family members, unable to find anyone until 1958 when Miriam was reunited with her aunts and grandmother.

Having relocated to Saigon with her mother and youngest aunt, Miriam attended the most privileged, elite school, ensuring that education remained a priority while her mother ran a textile business. Cultured and artistic, Miriam adored poetry, especially the celebrated poet Dinh Hung, who invited her to recite his poems on the radio one evening. Miriam's grandmother happened to hear her distinctive voice on the radio and insisted that she 'stop right now', adding: 'There will be no showgirl in our house!' Now, Miriam enjoys performing as the soprano with the Melbourne-based classical troupe Huong Xua, singing nostalgic Vietnamese music from the 1940s to 1960s.

Miriam was awarded a scholarship to study agriculture in Japan but her grandmother fell ill, so she declined the offer. Eventually she studied law, even though her family had demanded that she become a chemist. 'My family planned my future but I rebelled.' Her parents expected her to comply with an arranged marriage but Miriam met her first husband, an army lieutenant, at the Australian High Commission. 'He fell in love with me instantly but I made him wait five hours on our first date.'

Against the wishes of her family, they married in Saigon in March 1967 and arrived in Sydney in May. The adventurous couple travelled around the world for nine months before discovering in Las Vegas that Miriam was pregnant. Their son was born in 1968. They settled in Canberra where Miriam's husband was studying Economics. Miriam was soon cooking lunch at home for friends, sometimes sixty women, while busily knitting for three children. On one occasion, an Austrian Jew named Mrs Rosenberg gave her a lift to the Civic Centre. Miriam remembers feeling very comfortable in her company.

Miriam conducted cooking classes in Canberra, preparing spring rolls, chicken with lemongrass and beef with chilli. Tirelessly raising money for charity, she also cooked hundreds of spring rolls for the school fete. Her stall was so popular that she soon ran out of food. She began to prepare lamb chops and other Australian dishes, enjoying the abundant fresh produce at her disposal. Her daughters, Linda and Baci, love pho ga – chicken broth with shredded vermicelli, fish sauce and coriander. 'I like to cook for large crowds, with food shared and presented on platters. The more the merrier.'

Above Vietnamese Spring Rolls

Miriam Greenfield

After seventeen years in Canberra, the family moved to Melbourne in 1982, where they lived in the Jewish area of Caulfield, otherwise known as the 'bagel belt'. Feeling an innate connection to Judaism, Miriam attended the Temple Beth Israel on Friday nights with Rabbi John Levi when her children had fallen asleep. In 1984, Miriam returned to Vietnam to discover from her aunt what she had always suspected – that her father was part-Jewish. 'I always felt different,' she remembers. Miriam started to pursue Judaism – 'It's where I belong' – and her journey to an orthodox conversion began. Tragically, in 1988, she lost her husband and son within five months of each other. In 1990, she married Henry Greenfield, a Holocaust survivor, and now believes that destiny brought her into her current family.

Miriam can speak Hebrew, Vietnamese, French and English and understands Yiddish and German. She is committed to the Jewish charity WIZO Nirim and works as a phone counsellor for the Melbourne Sexual Health Centre. Her grandchildren, Ariella, Tali and Ben, are her pride and joy. Every Friday night, she cooks traditional Jewish food with chopsticks in one hand while frying her famous kosher chicken spring rolls with the other. She skilfully melds her disparate cuisines, nurturing her Jewish, Buddhist soul: 'I have a passion for cooking. One day I would love to have a restaurant. I am happiest when cooking up a storm.'

Vietnamese Spring Rolls

Cha Gio Chien

Miriam is famous for these kosher chicken spring rolls served on Friday nights.

500 kg (1 lb) minced chicken

250 g (9 oz) bean shoots, chopped

2 carrots, grated

1 onion, grated

2–3 cloves garlic, minced

1 tablespoon sugar

100 g (3½ oz) dry vermicelli noodles, cut into 2 cm (¾ in) pieces

2 eggs

salt

ground black pepper

40 square sheets spring roll pastry

1 egg white

canola oil for frying

iceberg lettuce

coriander, Vietnamese mint leaves, bean shoots or Vietnamese basil to garnish

Nuoc Mam

80 ml (3 fl oz) fish sauce

120 ml (4 fl oz) water

3 tablespoons sugar

juice of 2 limes

1 clove garlic, minced

1 red chilli, finely chopped

Mix the chicken, bean shoots, carrots, onion, garlic, sugar, noodles and eggs until well combined, then season. On a flat surface, lay out a single spring roll sheet in a diamond. Take 1 tablespoon of chicken mixture and lay it horizontally just below the centre of the diamond. Fold the bottom corner over the mixture and tuck it under as you fold both left and right sides into the centre. Continue rolling towards the top corner.

Beat the egg white and dab it onto the top corner of the spring roll to seal. This will ensure that the sheet holds its shape while frying. Repeat until all the filling has been used.

Heat the oil in a wok or deep frying pan until very hot. Add spring rolls in batches. Reduce the heat to medium and fry until golden brown. Spring rolls can be deep- or shallow-fried.

To make the nuoc mam, mix all the ingredients and set aside in a dipping bowl.

To serve, separate whole lettuce leaves and trim the tops so that they resemble cups. Place a hot spring roll in each cup with your garnish of choice and dip into the nuoc mam.

Makes 40

Vietnamese Rice Noodle Soup
Pho Ga

Miriam's daughters, Linda and Baci, love this soup made from chicken stock with shredded vermicelli, fish sauce and coriander.

1 packet (1 kg) fresh flat rice noodles

Chicken Stock

4 litres (7 pints) water

1 chicken

2 large onions

5 cm (2 in) piece ginger

4 star anise

1 tablespoon fish sauce

Garnish

slices of lemon or lime

Vietnamese basil

coriander

Vietnamese mint

spring onions, finely chopped

onion, finely sliced

bean shoots

red chilli, finely sliced

To make the stock, combine the water, chicken, onions, ginger, star anise and fish sauce in a saucepan, and bring to the boil. Reduce the heat and simmer on a low heat for 2 hours, skimming off any froth that rises to the surface. Chicken meat should be tender.

Remove the chicken breast from the chicken, slice finely and set aside. Return the remaining chicken to the stock. Simmer on a low heat for another hour. When cool, strain with a fine sieve so that the liquid is clear. Refrigerate the stock overnight and remove the layer of solidified fat that forms on the surface.

Rinse the noodles under boiling water in a colander. Ensure that the noodles do not become gluggy. To serve, place a small amount of rice noodles in a bowl with some chicken breast and garnish of choice, then cover with boiling stock. Additional garnishes can be served alongside the soup.

Serves 12

Miriam Greenfield

Vietnamese Beef Salad

Gỏi Bò

1 tablespoon sesame oil

2 tablespoons mirin or rice wine

1 clove garlic, minced

2 eye fillet steaks

1 carrot, grated

1 Lebanese cucumber, deseeded and peeled into fine strips

1 red onion, finely sliced or grated

200 g (7 oz) bean shoots

1 red capsicum, peeled into fine strips

1 tablespoon shredded ginger

½ bunch mint

½ bunch coriander

½ cup roasted peanuts, crushed

2 red chillies, finely sliced

chopped coriander to garnish

Nuoc Mam (see page 123)

Combine the sesame oil, mirin and garlic. Add the fillets and marinate for at least 4 hours.

Fry the fillets in a non-stick frying pan until medium rare. Allow them to cool, then cut against the grain into fine slices. Mix the remaining ingredients in a bowl and add fillet slices.

To make the nuoc mam, see page 123. Toss through the salad, garnish with additional coriander and serve at room temperature.

Serves 4

Sticky Coconut Rice Pudding

Chuối Nếp Chưng Nước Dừa

2 cups gluten rice (sticky rice)

1 cup water

800 ml (27 fl oz) coconut milk

¼ cup sugar

2 tablespoons sugar, extra

4 bananas or 4 slices mango

1 tablespoon butter

2 tablespoons roasted sesame seeds

Put the rice, water, 400 ml (13½ fl oz) coconut milk and ¼ cup sugar in a rice cooker for about 20 minutes, until the rice is cooked. (Alternatively, add rice, water, milk and sugar to a saucepan. Bring to the boil and simmer on a low heat for 20 minutes, until the rice is tender.)

Fill 4 ramekin dishes, 5 cm (2 in) in diameter, with rice mixture and set aside. The ramekins will mould the rice into individual puddings.

Heat 400 ml (13½ fl oz) coconut milk and 2 tablespoons sugar in a saucepan and stir on a medium heat until the sugar dissolves.

Peel the bananas and slice in half lengthwise. Heat the butter in a frying pan, add the bananas and fry them until they are golden brown on both sides.

To serve, heat the ramekins in the microwave for 1 minute or leave cold and invert onto a plate. Place 2 cooked banana halves beside the rice pudding. Pour the hot coconut sauce over the dessert and garnish with sesame seeds.

Serves 4

Africa

Libya, Morocco, South Africa, Zimbabwe

Jews living in the countries of Africa introduced into their cooking the new flavours they encountered there. Following a North African and Italian tradition, Libyan cuisine has acquired exotic tastes and blended flavours; Moroccan cooking features both Arabic and French aspects, exemplified by fragrant couscous. In contrast, the Jews of South Africa and Zimbabwe have interpreted traditional dishes to incorporate the zesty flavours of Portugal and heavy glazes for barbecues.

Dina Goldschlager LIBYA

I find cooking therapeutic and nourishing. I am an adventurous cook and never follow recipes. With Sephardi food, you can make something out of nothing. A kilo of semolina can be transformed into a banquet for ten people. I have neat and quick cooking methods. Luckily, my four children always enjoyed eating, so I could experiment.

DINA Goldschlager has a precious Jewish Italian cookbook that belonged to her late mother, Rina Maimon, its cover adorned with a black and white photograph of Rina, surrounded by tiny red beads in the shape of a heart. The book contains a calendar of meals that revolve around Jewish festivals – Sephardi delicacies that Rina prepared every year as well as the individual bread rolls that she lovingly baked for each of her children, inscribed with their initials, for holy days. For Dina, the book symbolises the origins of her love of cooking.

Born in Tripoli in 1950, Dina is the youngest of four children. As Libya was an Italian colony until 1943, the family spoke Italian at home and identified with Italian culture. Her mother was a direct descendant of Maimonides, the eleventh-century doctor, scholar and philosopher. Her grandmother, Gullia, was best friends with an aristocratic girl, Nana, thought to be a princess. Nana warned her to take her family and escape Libya as there were troubled times brewing for Jews. Many Libyan Jews were affluent and there was a festering undercurrent of anti-Semitism.

Dina's maternal grandfather, Isaac, was a successful merchant while her uncle David was an agent for Johnnie Walker and Maserati cars. He owned racehorses and movie theatres. Every Sunday, Rina and some of her siblings would drive around Libya with their father and a chauffeur. Tragically, on one occasion they had a car accident and Dina's grandfather and his youngest child died. Rina's mother was in hospital for six months with two broken legs. When Rina was just sixteen, she and her brother had to manage the family's business.

On the other side of her family, Dina's deeply orthodox, paternal grandfather, Shabtai, came to live with the family. He prayed three times a day in the synagogue and embroidered Torah covers, tallits (prayer shawls) and Arabic caftans with silver and gold threads. For Dina, 'his room was fascinating.'

In 1948, Dina's uncle Clem went to Israel as a volunteer in the air force and in 1951 Dina's family followed him, selling some valuable commodities to survive the tough times. At first, the family lived in a pre-fabricated house in Pardes Katz – a district populated by migrants from Spain, Bulgaria and Iraq, to name a few. Her mother now cooked on a tiny burner in impoverished conditions that were a far cry from her former life of luxury. Then, they moved to a flat in Tel-Giborim near Ramat-Gan.

iumo dell'atàr di T

costretto alla fuga nel '67 ricorda

L'ALBUM
DI UNA VITA
Prima della paura

IN LIBIA
Il lungomare di Tripoli
negli anni '60 (sono...
Accanto, mamma e...
bambini ebrei che...
assistono a una...
di calcio a Tripo...
centro una zia...
Victor Magiar...
due cuginett...
e Moshe. A...
uno scorci...
con l'arc...
Marc'Au...
sfondo...

Rina, although working in a hospital to help support the family, still prepared couscous in advance for the Sabbath every week. Following a North African and Italian tradition, she pickled vegetables, partly so they wouldn't require refrigeration. While helping polish silver and clean furniture, Dina watched her mother cook.

Their large extended family attended sumptuous Sephardi feasts on Friday nights at Rina's or her mother's home. Rice, chickpeas, lima and borlotti beans were typical ingredients, while legumes were plentiful. For dessert, they enjoyed fruit salad and semolina cake called safra – Rina's recipe that all family members can bake. In Israel, Dina's aunt Ilda and uncle Clem would visit on Saturdays for lunch. The rowdy family would gather to sing opera songs and tell stories.

In 1959, Clem migrated to Sydney with Ilda, as life was too difficult in Israel. Ilda was like a sister to Rina and both taught Dina to cook. Progressively, Dina's two older brothers migrated to Sydney after they completed training in the Israeli army. Finally, Dina, at the age of fifteen, travelled with her mother and brother, Moshe, to Sydney in 1966. At first, the family lived in North Bondi while their mother worked in a handbag factory. Her two older brothers started a petrol station while her younger brother became a fashion agent.

When Dina finished high school, she visited Melbourne with a friend, Diane, and met Ronny, a young engineering student. They courted for three years while Dina was completing her architectural studies in Sydney. Married in 1972, the couple lived in a rented flat in Armadale while Dina worked in an architectural office in Box Hill. She found the separation from her mother challenging. In 1974, Dina's first son, Tony, was born but sadly, when he was three months old, Rina passed away. Ilda became a second mother, caring for the family and always teaching Dina new dishes, such as charred and preserved spinach cooked with lima beans.

Dina's family is dispersed throughout Venice, Florence, Rome, Paris and Israel, but she enjoys cooking for the family she has in Australia, in particular, for her four children, Tony, Sharonne, Tammy and Dalia. Just like her mother, Dina loves roasting pistachios, almonds and cashews over a fire. She continues the tradition of Sabbath meals in her home, cooking a great variety of vegetable dishes, thereby maintaining her distinctive Sephardi and Italian heritage.

Above Safra

Pickled Vegetables

Sephardi Jews prepare a big dish of these vegetables on Friday and eat them with all meals over the Sabbath.

2 teaspoons rock salt

½ cup boiling water

juice of 2 lemons

1 carrot

¼ cauliflower, cut into florets

½ kohlrabi, cut into chunks

½ turnip, cut into chunks

2 stalks celery

1 fennel, thickly sliced

In a glass dish, mix the salt, water and lemon juice. Cut the carrot in half lengthwise and then cut each half into 6 pieces.

Place all the vegetables in the lemon water. Mix well, turning the vegetables a few times. Marinate for 3 hours. Refrigerate and serve.

Serves 8–10

Rice Salad

2 tablespoons sunflower oil

2 cups basmati rice

4 cups water

1 teaspoon salt

1 Lebanese cucumber, finely chopped

2 tomatoes, finely chopped

½ red onion, finely chopped

¼ bunch continental parsley, finely chopped

1 x 300 g can chickpeas

¼ cup roasted sunflower seeds or pistachios

DRESSING

½ cup olive oil

¼ cup balsamic vinegar

1 tablespoon sesame oil

½ tablespoon soy sauce or tamari

1 clove garlic, minced

pinch of salt

¼ teaspoon ground black pepper

Heat the oil in a saucepan, pour in the rice and stir for a few minutes so that it absorbs the flavour of the oil. Add the water and salt. Bring to the boil and simmer, covered, for 20–25 minutes, until the water has been absorbed and the rice is soft. Fluff the rice with a fork and set aside to cool.

Add the remaining salad ingredients and stir to combine.

Combine the dressing ingredients, mix well and pour over the salad.

Serves 8

Meatballs

This dish was brought to Italy by the Sephardim who fled the Spanish Inquisition in the 1490s. It is also found in Arabic cooking and is traditionally accompanied by couscous.

SAUCE

1 x 440 g can tomato purée

3 cans water

3 tablespoons tomato paste

3 tablespoons sugar

1 teaspoon ground cumin

1 teaspoon salt

$^1/_2$ teaspoon ground black pepper

MEATBALLS

1 kg (2 lb) minced meat (veal, beef, chicken or a combination of any two)

$^1/_4$ cup finely chopped parsley

2 cloves garlic, minced

2 eggs, beaten

$^1/_2$ cup basmati rice, washed

1 teaspoon salt

$^1/_2$ teaspoon ground black pepper

Bring all the sauce ingredients to a boil in a saucepan and then simmer on a low heat for 15–20 minutes.

While the sauce is simmering, combine all the meatball ingredients in a large bowl. Wearing rubber gloves, roll the meat into balls and gently drop into the sauce. Cook the meatballs, covered, on a medium heat for about 1 hour.

Serves 8–10

Chicken with Chickpeas

Chickpeas are synonymous with Arabic cooking. This is a tasty and easy dish. Gravy beef or osso bucco may be substituted for chicken. Beans may be substituted for chickpeas.

2 cups chickpeas

4 tablespoons tomato paste

2 cups water

1 chicken, skinned and cut into 8 pieces

1 tablespoon ground cumin

1 teaspoon ground cinnamon

1 teaspoon salt

$^1/_2$ teaspoon ground black pepper

Soak the chickpeas in water overnight or microwave in 4 cups of water for about 20 minutes.

Heat the tomato paste in a saucepan on a medium heat and gradually add the water, stirring until well combined. When the sauce begins to simmer, add the chickpeas and cook, covered, for about 15 minutes.

Add the chicken and spices. Adjust seasoning to taste. Cook, covered, for 30 minutes, until the chicken is cooked and the chickpeas are soft. Serve with rice, Israeli couscous or regular couscous.

Serves 8

Opposite Rice Salad

Non-dairy Tiramisu

With the Italian occupation of Libya in 1911 many Italian dishes were adapted. The use of nuts and parve cream is an interesting variation. Tiramisu can be made a few days in advance. However, the cream should be applied on the day of serving.

6 egg yolks

½ cup sugar

200 g (7 oz) ground almonds or walnuts

120 g (4 oz) instant coffee

2 cups boiling water

300 g (11 oz) thin sponge finger biscuits

400 ml (14 fl oz) parve cream

½ cup caster sugar

150 g (5 oz) dark chocolate, grated

Beat the egg yolks, sugar, almonds and 2 tablespoons of coffee to form a thick paste. If the paste is too thick to spread, add a little cold water.

Combine the remaining coffee with boiling water and allow to cool. Quickly soak the biscuits in the coffee and arrange them along the bottom of a 24 cm (9½ in) square dish. Spread the nut mixture over the biscuits and top with another layer of coffee-soaked biscuits.

Whip the cream with sugar to form soft peaks. Spread the cream over the top of biscuits and top with grated chocolate. Refrigerate and serve.

Serves 8–10

Semolina Cake
Safra

For dessert, Dina's family enjoy fruit salad and this semolina cake, called safra. Her mother's recipe, it was shared with all the family members and is now a favourite of Dina's grandchildren.

200 g (7 oz) pitted dates

3 eggs

½ cup sugar

1 cup water or orange juice

¾ cup vegetable oil

1 teaspoon vanilla essence

1 teaspoon baking powder

3 cups semolina

20 almonds

SYRUP

1 cup sugar

1 cup water

1 teaspoon ground cinnamon

¼ cup honey

Preheat the oven to 160°C (320°F). Line a 20 cm (8 in) square baking tin with baking paper.

Boil the dates in a saucepan with water for 10 minutes or microwave dates in water for 8 minutes. Set aside to cool.

Beat the eggs with the sugar, water, oil, vanilla essence and baking powder until well combined. Gradually add the semolina to form a loose consistency. Drain the dates and add them to the semolina, then pour the mixture into the baking tin. Arrange the almonds in lines on top of the cake mixture. Bake for 30 minutes, until golden brown.

To prepare the syrup, boil the sugar, water and cinnamon in a saucepan for 20 minutes. Remove from heat and add honey.

Cut the cake into 10 cm (4 in) squares. Pour the syrup over the cake. The cake will absorb all the syrup. Serve warm or cool.

Serves 12–14

Africa, Libya

Opposite Non-dairy Tiramisu

Eva Keinan MOROCCO

I grew up in quite primitive and segregated conditions in a mud house with water from a central fountain. From the age of seven, my sister Solange and I cooked for our entire family. My family was poor, but we were rich in our cultural way of life, with strong communal feelings.

BORN in 1945 in the small village of Demnat, Eva grew up in a large family with eight children, all of whom spoke a Moroccan Jewish dialect at home. Their sheltered upbringing revolved around celebrations and rituals within the Jewish calendar. They kept a fully kosher home, with separate milk and meat. Her father, Yamin, owned a small fruit and vegetable store that was just one by two metres while her mother, Yacot, busily ran a sewing business for Arabs. When Eva was five, her family of four sisters and three brothers moved to Marrakesh. Initially, they lived in Mellah, the Jewish quarter, which allowed proximity to centres of Jewish life – the synagogue, kosher butcher and ritual baths. Their home shared a central courtyard with neighbouring families, which was a hub for community life.

Eva's two older sisters were already married at the age of thirteen and fourteen and lived nearby. As a young girl, Eva watched them cook with her mother. Then, from the age of seven, while her parents were working she prepared meals for her family, helped by her younger sister, Solange. As soon as Eva returned home from school each day, she would start to cook for the family.

With no written recipes, she prepared fish, vegetables and couscous from a clay oven heated with coals. For the Sabbath feast and Passover, the women cooked together and Eva was able to prepare her own matzo from the age of eight. For large festivals, members of the close-knit Jewish community gathered to cook, sharing anecdotes, stories and aspirations.

Ratatouille was Eva's father's favourite dish, along with fish or chicken cooked in a tagine, and omelettes. Olives and salads accompanied most meals. Typical spices included cumin, coriander, turmeric and saffron. Many of the Jewish dishes were enlivened with red paprika and black pepper; sweet dishes would typically be enhanced with cinnamon. Eva also discovered the nuances of Arabic cooking from Fatima, a local woman who helped the family with their cooking and cleaning. Elaborately presented for festive occasions, the table was laden with immense colour and variety, and each dish was imbued with a combination of different spices.

For the Sabbath, the family cooked cholent from chickpeas, barley, rice, sweet potatoes, eggs, meat, nuts and dried fruits. All ingredients were combined in a gigantic pot which was then taken to the local Arab bakery for cooking on Friday and, since Jews cannot use fire on the Sabbath, collected on Saturday afternoon after it had been cooking in the oven for many hours. Every Friday, paprika would be finely ground to accompany various dishes. Early in the morning, Eva's mother prepared

Turkish bread, which she would also take to the bakery. Sometimes, Eva's father would leave work early to assist with cooking, especially with the meat or fish balls. Refreshing mint tea was served with beautifully decorated biscuits, completing any delicious feast.

When Eva was twelve, the family moved to the French quarter and she attended Alliance Française High School. When Morocco gained independence, she studied classical Arabic. In 1960, the family spent two years in transition in Casablanca, as part of the process of migrating to Israel. When Eva finished high school she worked as a teacher for underprivileged children. Then she migrated to Israel, living in Nazareth for two years before settling in Kiryat Gat, near Ashkelon. Eva was sponsored to undertake social work at Jerusalem University where she completed a postgraduate degree in rehabilitation. In Israel, Eva married a Sephardi who was active in local political movements, and they had two children.

In 1973, Eva emigrated to Melbourne where her two brothers had settled. She worked as a social worker but now owns a fashion store. Even though there is a small Moroccan Jewish community in Melbourne, Eva longs to maintain her Jewish cultural traditions. She attends the Sephardi synagogue and has taught her daughter to prepare Moroccan delicacies. 'I have many nostalgic memories from long ago which I relive with passion and desire. I crave Moroccan heritage and tradition. One day, I want to furnish my house in a Moroccan style.' Eva doesn't measure ingredients or use recipes; instead she cooks by improvising and estimating. The result is a delectable fusion of flavours and spices.

Above Moroccan Spicy Fish

Ratatouille

This colourful dish reflects the French influence on Moroccan cuisine.

2 eggplants, cubed
salt
½ cup water
2 red capsicums, cubed
4 tomatoes, cubed
½ clove garlic
1 tablespoon ground turmeric
1 tablespoon sweet or hot paprika
1 tablespoon ground black pepper
1 tablespoon salt

Salt the eggplants until they sweat. Rinse and pat dry with a paper towel. Heat the water in a large saucepan and add all the ingredients. Bring to the boil and then simmer for 30 minutes, until vegetables are soft. Serve at room temperature.

Serves 8–10

Moroccan Spicy Fish

1 kg (2 lb) snapper, mullet, trevally or sea perch
1 tablespoon sea salt
juice of 1 lemon
6 carrots, quartered
½ bunch parsley, roughly chopped
1 clove garlic, finely sliced
1 tablespoon ground turmeric
2 tablespoons sweet paprika
1 teaspoon ground black pepper
6–8 small red chillies
½ cup olive oil
½ cup water
1 bunch coriander, finely chopped, to garnish

Wash and pat dry the fish. Cut into cutlets, keeping the head and tail intact. Rub the fish with salt and lemon juice and allow to rest for 10 minutes.

Place the carrots and parsley at the bottom of a deep saucepan. Set the fish on top and add the garlic.

Mix the spices with the oil and pour over the fish. Add water, ensuring the fish is covered.

Cover the saucepan and bring to the boil. Simmer for about 30 minutes. Transfer the fish to a platter and serve hot or at room temperature. Garnish with fresh coriander.

Serves 6

Chicken Tagine

A tagine is a conical clay vessel used for preparing hearty casseroles. The combination of meat or poultry with dried fruit is typical of Moroccan cuisine.

1 chicken, cut into 10 pieces

juice of ½ lemon

2 teaspoons chicken stock powder

500 g (1 lb) dried apricots

500 g (1 lb) pitted prunes

½ teaspoon ground black pepper

120 g (4 oz) honey

Preheat the oven to 150°C (300°F).

Wash and pat dry the chicken, then rub it with lemon juice and stock powder.

Place all the ingredients in a tagine or a baking dish and cover with foil. Bake in the oven for 1 hour.

Mix the ingredients and bake for another hour, uncovered.

Serves 5

Moroccan Couscous with Beef and Vegetables

The turmeric in this dish gives the couscous a rich, golden colour.

¼ cup olive oil

3 brown onions, roughly chopped

1 kg (2 lb) beef spare ribs

1 teaspoon ground turmeric

1 teaspoon ground black pepper

1 teaspoon salt

6 carrots, quartered

¼ butternut pumpkin, roughly chopped

1 x 440 g can chickpeas

Couscous

120 ml (4 fl oz) olive oil

1 teaspoon ground turmeric

2 teaspoons chicken stock powder

1 teaspoon salt

1 teaspoon ground black pepper

1 kg (2 lb) couscous

Heat the oil in a large saucepan and sauté the onions until brown, stirring at regular intervals. Add the beef and seal until browned on both sides. Add the turmeric, pepper and salt. Pour boiling water over the meat to cover. Cook on a low heat for about 1 hour, until meat is tender.

Add the chopped vegetables to the saucepan and cook for a further 30 minutes. Add the chickpeas.

To prepare the couscous, in a separate saucepan combine the oil, turmeric, stock powder, salt and pepper. Mix the couscous into the oil and spices, and cover with boiling water. Cover the saucepan with a lid so that there are no gaps. Allow the couscous to rest for 30 minutes, stirring at regular intervals with a fork to prevent lumps and glugginess.

Serve the couscous on a platter and place the meat and vegetables on top. Ladle some of the sauce over the couscous.

Serves 10

Opposite Ratatouille

June Edelmuth SOUTH AFRICA

*Australia is the haven of Jews from all over the world –
each immigrant bringing their own family recipes and
traditions, the end product often looking and tasting very
different. South Africans have a different interpretation of
Jewish dishes. We eat kreplach and chicken soup to start
the fast, warm boolkes to break the fast, flomien tzimmes
at the Passover seder and Bobba's thick vegetable soup
with chunks of meat and marrow bones on Shabbes.
These are just some of the traditions I will pass on
to my children. Until my arrival in Australia,
honey cake was foreign in my home.*

BORN in Johannesburg in 1952, June was the first of three children. Their family home was in the predominantly Jewish suburb of Greenside, where June attended lessons in Hebrew and Jewish studies with her younger sister, Elana, and brother Ronny. Judaism flourished in their kosher home. Often more than fifty guests – June's vast extended family – attended the Sabbath banquet. June's mother worked diligently until the early hours of the morning – baking, kneading and preparing her delicacies that were treasured by family members. Like her mother, June bakes numerous cakes – strudels, crème puffs and chiffon cakes.

June's mother, Bertha, arrived in South Africa at the age of twelve from Russia with her older sister Sonia and younger sister Lily. Bertha cooked delicious cheese cake, potato kugel and teiglach – a biscuit mixture boiled in syrup so it is coated in a crunchy, caramel texture; Lily prepared kichel (biscuits), chopped herring and liver while Sonia was renowned for chicken soup, kneidlach and perogen – meat blintzes made with minced cow's lung. June gathered the recipes for the three cookbooks she has written by spending hours observing her mother and aunts cooking family dishes. Recording their prized recipes and secrets, she has transformed 'a little bit of this, a little bit of that' into successful recipe books, thereby preserving her distinctive heritage.

At university, June completed a degree in teaching, majoring in French and Afrikaans – a language derived from Dutch that is spoken in southern Africa, primarily in South Africa, Zimbabwe and Namibia. In 1973, she married Steve Edelmuth whose parents were from Germany. Industrious and energetic, June started a successful cookery and creative sewing school, teaching appliqué, patchwork

and smocking, as well as a catering company with her sister, Elana, and sister-in-law, Dana. The catering company flourished in South Africa for ten years from 1990 to 2000. She catered for functions attended by the King of Swaziland, the Premier of Gauteng and Nelson Mandela, all while caring for her four children – Richard, Carly, Gregory and Ryan. Fortunately, June had the help of a live-in maid and housekeeper as well as a gardener, who were like 'substitute parents, adored and respected by all'. Her children enjoyed eating mielie pap, a hearty stew made from maize and short rib, with tomato gravy.

Family outings included visits to wild game parks such as the Kruger National Park and Sabi Sabi. Eating rusks on early morning game drives, open air braais (barbecues) in the bush and cooking boerewors (a spicy South African sausage) were part of their lifestyle. Thick, rich marinades abound in South African cooking, giving meat a glaze when grilled on a barbecue. Mrs Ball's chutney – famous in South Africa – is an essential ingredient.

Growing up with apartheid touched all aspects of life in South Africa, with every home surrounded by a high wall and barbed wire. When June was teaching in a primary school in the Johannesburg suburb of Montrose in 1977, she vividly recalls looking past the end of the corridor to see the billowing plumes of smoke oppressively hanging over Soweto. As time progressed, crime increased and the family felt more and more unsafe.

June arrived in Sydney in 2000 when her husband purchased Cherry Bim, a renowned Jewish catering company. Within a short time, their house in South Africa was sold as they awaited migration papers. This rapid decision was at once thrilling and unsettling. June arrived with her children in January, stayed in a hotel room for one week, then moved into an empty house in Sydney as their furniture hadn't arrived. Soon, June was conducting her popular cooking courses from home while devising menus and sourcing recipes for the catering company.

June relishes the freshness and quality of ingredients available in Sydney, which may have contributed to a simplification of her cooking. A swift cook, June enjoys preparing stir-fries as well as barbecues, integrating Asian vegetables and herbs such as coriander, mint and lemongrass into her extensive repertoire.

Above *Malva Pudding*

Low-fat Granola

4 cups rolled oats

4½ cups Sultana Bran

2 cups Rice Bubbles

600 g (1¼ lb) assorted nuts, coarsely
chopped

200 g (7 oz) flaked almonds

1 cup dried apricots, figs and dates,
chopped

⅓ cup oil

2 cups honey

⅓ cup brown sugar

½ cup orange juice

Preheat the oven to 170°C (340°F).

Combine the cereals, nuts and dried fruits. Heat the oil, honey and sugar, and add to the cereal mixture. Add orange juice and mix until well coated.

Line two or three baking trays with baking paper. Spoon the mixture onto the trays (do not pile mixture onto one tray, as it will not roast evenly). Bake for 40–60 minutes, until golden. Toss every 20 minutes to prevent burning.

Remove from the oven and cool. Store in an airtight container.

Makes about 2 kg (4 lb)

Strawberry Fields Salad

'In South African cuisine, salads accompany all meals. The appearance of fruit and nuts in a salad is very common. Strawberry Fields Salad is one of my favourite recipes. The taste is sensational and the colours are visually so appealing.'

700 g (1½ lb) mesclun salad mix or
baby spinach

2 punnets strawberries, quartered

1 punnet blueberries

½ cucumber, deseeded and sliced

handful of snow peas, cut diagonally

1 red onion, sliced or
½ cup chopped spring onions

1 avocado, sliced

300 g (11 oz) caramelised or smoked
almonds

DRESSING

¾ cup vegetable oil

¾ cup apple cider vinegar

100 g (3½ oz) brown sugar

1 teaspoon salt

½ teaspoon ground black pepper

a few drops of Tabasco sauce

Combine all the salad ingredients except the almonds. Whisk the dressing ingredients and, just before serving, dress the salad and top with nuts.

Serves 8–10

Opposite (left to right) Low-fat Granola and South African Rusks

Steakhouse Marinade

Thick, rich marinades abound in South African cooking, giving meat a glaze when grilled on a barbecue.

20 g (²/₃ oz) instant coffee

1 cup vegetable oil

30 g (1 oz) crushed garlic

13 g (¹/₃ oz) finely chopped ginger

15 g (¹/₂ oz) ground black pepper

15 g (¹/₂ oz) mustard powder

3 teaspoons Ina Paarman's Braai and Grill* (barbecue seasoning)

3 teaspoons dried parsley

1¹/₂ cups tomato sauce

1¹/₂ cups barbecue sauce

1¹/₂ cups Ms Ball's Chutney* (peach chutney)

¹/₂ cup lemon juice

³/₄ cup soy sauce

1–2 tablespoons Maleney's chilli jam (Australian addition to recipe)

Mix the coffee with 1 tablespoon of water. Combine all the ingredients. This marinade should be used to marinate steak and chops for 3–4 days and chicken overnight before barbecuing.

Marinade for 8 small or 6 large steaks

Available from stores that stock South African products

Malva Pudding

2 eggs

2 cups sugar

2 tablespoons apricot jam

2 cups flour

pinch of salt

2 teaspoons bicarbonate of soda

1¹/₂ tablespoons butter

2 teaspoons vinegar

2 cups milk

icing sugar for dusting

SAUCE

400 ml (14 fl oz) cream

³/₄ cup butter

1¹/₂ cups sugar

2 teaspoons vanilla essence

³/₄ cup boiling water

Preheat the oven to 170°C (340°F).

Beat the eggs and sugar until frothy. Add the jam and beat again.

Sift the flour, salt and bicarbonate of soda into a separate bowl. Melt the butter and then add vinegar to it. Pour the butter into the egg mixture, then add the milk, alternating with the dry ingredients. Beat well.

Grease a 3 litre (5 pint) baking dish. Pour the mixture into the dish and bake for 30 minutes. Cover with foil, shiny side up, and bake for a further 25–30 minutes, until a skewer comes out clean.

Combine all the sauce ingredients and heat until the butter melts. Pour it over the pudding as soon as you remove it from the oven. Prick the pudding to help the sauce seep in.

The pudding can be made in advance and frozen. Heat, covered with foil, for about 30 minutes, until hot. Serve dusted with icing sugar.

Serves 12–15

Africa, South Africa

Sweet Biscuits

Kichel

1½ cups flour, sifted

1 teaspoon baking powder

¼ cup sugar

3 eggs, beaten

¼ cup vegetable oil

sugar for sprinkling

Preheat the oven to 200°C (400°F).

Place the flour, baking powder and sugar in a bowl. Make a well in the centre and add the eggs and oil. Beat well.

Divide the dough into three pieces. If it is sticky, knead in a little extra flour. Roll it out very thinly (if you have a pasta machine, push it through the machine). Brush the dough sparingly with oil and sprinkle generously with sugar. Press the sugar down slightly with a rolling pin. Cut the dough into rectangular shapes about 6 cm x 10 cm (2½ in x 4 in). Line a baking tray with baking paper, place the shapes on the tray and bake for 6–8 minutes. (Watch carefully, as kichel burn very quickly.) Store in an airtight container.

Makes about 50

South African Rusks

'Descended from the Dutch rusk, these are a cross between the French biscuit and the German Zwieback. They last a long time and I remember munching on them on long family drives.'

1 kg (2 lb) self-raising flour

350 g (12½ oz) Sultana Bran

125 g (4 oz) sultanas

100 g (3½ oz) chopped dates

1 cup sunflower seeds

100 g (3½ oz) chopped pecans

½ cup desiccated coconut

50 g (1½ oz) sesame seeds

1½ tablespoons poppy seeds

1½ tablespoons baking powder

250 g (9 oz) brown sugar

2 cups buttermilk

2 cups melted butter

2 eggs, beaten

Preheat the oven to 170°C (340°F). Place all the ingredients in a large bowl and mix with a wooden spoon.

Line two 23 cm x 33 cm (9 in x 13 in) lamington tins with baking paper. Spoon the mixture into the trays and press down slightly with your hands. Bake for 45 minutes. Remove from the oven, cut into 3 cm x 8 cm (1½ in x 3 in) slices and cool.

Reduce the oven temperature to 75°C–100°C (150°F–200°F). Spread out the slices on baking paper and return to the oven. Leave overnight to dry out.

Makes 60

June Edelmuth

Cinnamon Buns
Boolkes

June enjoys cooking her mother's precious recipe for boolkes – a cinnamon and raisin bun with yeast, served warm to break the fast of Yom Kippur.

50 g (1½ oz) fresh yeast

½ cup lukewarm water

1½ cups sugar, plus ¼ teaspoon extra

1 teaspoon salt, plus ¼ teaspoon extra

250 g (9 oz) butter

¼ cup margarine

150 ml (5 fl oz) milk

150 ml (5 fl oz) cream

6½ cups plain flour

4 eggs

1 egg yolk

a little oil for spraying

FILLING

2½ cups sugar

5 tablespoons ground cinnamon

¾ cup melted butter for brushing

handful of sultanas

2 eggs, beaten

STREUSEL TOPPING

1 cup plain flour

100 g (3½ oz) butter

100 g (3½ oz) sugar

Crumble the yeast into a small bowl. Add the water, ¼ teaspoon sugar and ¼ teaspoon salt. Cover the bowl with plastic wrap and leave it in a warm place until very frothy.

Melt the butter and margarine, but do not boil. Add the milk and cream, and set aside.

Sift the flour, sugar and salt together. Beat the eggs with the extra yolk until frothy. Add the flour mixture to the eggs, then add the yeast mixture. Beat with a dough hook for 10–12 minutes, or knead by hand. Place the dough in a bowl that has been sprayed with oil, and cover with plastic. Leave it in a warm place until the dough doubles in bulk, about 6 hours, depending on the weather.

Throw the dough onto a floured board, divide into three and knead each piece. Add as little flour as possible, as it will only make the dough heavy. Knead as little as possible, as it spoils the texture. The dough must be just manageable. Ensure there is a little flour on the rolling pin and roll each piece of dough out until about 20 cm (8 in) wide and 5 mm (¼ in) thick.

Make the cinnamon sugar by combining the sugar and cinnamon. Brush the dough generously with melted butter, sprinkle liberally with cinnamon sugar and sultanas, and roll up lengthwise. Cut the log into 5 cm (2 in) sections and place in the cups of large muffin tins, sliced side up. Mix the beaten eggs with a little water and brush the top of the dough.

Mix the streusel ingredients and sprinkle generously on top. Leave to prove or increase in bulk for about 2 hours.

Preheat the oven to 180°C (350°F).

Bake for about 20 minutes. Boolkes freeze well. Reheat, covered in foil.

Makes 40

Delia & Lana Raizon ZIMBABWE

We grew up watching, tasting, smelling, talking, feeling and experiencing life in our mother's well-loved kitchen. We are self-taught, self-confessed foodies. We think of food with passion and insist that the art of cooking involves a very special ingredient – love. Love for food and love for those you invite to your table.

DELIA AND LANA Raizon were born in Bulawayo, Zimbabwe, in a home surrounded by a massive garden abundant with avocado and lemon trees as well as grenadilla vines. Both sisters remember the smells of fresh produce engulfing their home.

As children, they would come home to savour a hearty African peasant stew: 'My fondest childhood memories are of rushing home from school to join our African staff for lunch,' Delia reflects. 'The stew they made was cooked in a large cast-iron pot over an open fire. It was served with a large pot of sadza, which is white maize meal, similar to polenta, boiled until it thickens enough to form little balls in your fingers. Wilted wild greens were served with it. The meal was eaten outdoors under a tree. Sitting in a circle on the floor, the pots were placed in the centre and we all dipped in.' Africans use beans as they are cheap and plentiful, making the stew deliciously thick and high in protein. Of course, the girls were unable to eat their dinner afterwards!

Delia and Lana enjoyed baking with their grandmother, Vera Bernstein – layered jellies, trifles, jam tarts, melting moments and stuffed monkeys (biscuits filled with fruit and nuts, then cut into slices). For Delia, 'Vera had the ability to make something out of nothing. She could cook an amazing concoction of dishes, especially her famous pies.' Over time, Delia and Lana's mother, Sandy, has transcribed Vera's precious recipes, especially her traditional Jewish dishes – gefilte fish, chicken soup, roast chicken and chopped liver.

Vera was also talented at sewing, knitting and crocheting – filling ice-cream containers to the brim with buttons and lace. She sewed her own clothes and adorned herself with brooches and beads. Delia cooked with her on the hot patio while her mother worked in a clothing factory, designing children's garments. Lana would make gift cards close by. Their grandmother enjoyed preparing 'comfort food' such as casseroles, stews, curries, sweet and sour fish and cottage pie. She would also stuff peppers with meat left over from a previous barbecue and had imaginative ways to occupy the

sisters while something was cooking in the oven. Meanwhile, their industrious grandfather, Abe, was building furniture, fixing electrical equipment, welding and deploying his technical skills. The 'taste of food was important to him. He always said "nothing is as good as her cooking". He never let any of it go to waste.'

Before 1980, Zimbabwe was an English colony known as Rhodesia. The country shared a border with Mozambique, a Portuguese colony, so the family's cooking has been influenced by both English traditions (such as afternoon tea) and Portuguese (peri peri chicken).

On Friday nights, Delia and Lana went to their grandmother's flamboyant house with its red velvet carpet and purple room with opulent wallpaper. There, she cooked fried fish, chicken soup and kreplach, homemade chopped liver and roast chicken. With a keen attention to detail in her presentation, Vera even baked her own challah bread, called kitkah in South Africa. To break the fast of Yom Kippur, she baked babkas – chocolate yeast buns. She also prepared herring dip mixed with Maree biscuits. For special occasions, Vera baked cakes loved for their kitschness – covered in blue icing with silver baubles.

In 1977, Lana, aged seven, and Delia, aged five, migrated with their mother to Australia, following their father Ian, who had secured work buying fabrics for a Swiss company based in Melbourne. It was an intensely emotional farewell as they left their beloved grandparents. On the plane to Australia, Sandy, Lana and Delia were petrified when one of the engines caught fire and plumes of smoke billowed from under the wing. They hurried back to Johannesburg after this false start. When the family eventually arrived in Melbourne, Lana and Delia were enrolled in the local primary school, where, they recall, 'the tuck shop sold eucalyptus lollies and meat pies'.

Food has always been a central focus for the family and in earlier days the walk-in pantry was constantly filled with the whirring sound of the mixmaster as cakes, toffees and sweets were produced. These days, the family enjoys 'cook-ups', testing and trying new recipes. Sabbath and festivals are prepared with a combined effort, served in hand-thrown pottery from Zimbabwe while fine, floral-patterned Royal Doulton bone china is used for English afternoon teas. Delia makes fresh salads and Lana bakes cakes and desserts, while Sandy cooks soups.

Sandy recalls buying expensive mangoes and avocados when the family first settled in Melbourne. She loved kiwi fruit and once filled a bag with them, mistakenly thinking that the price was per kilogram rather than for each fruit. Sandy catered for her daughters' bat mitzvahs, ensuring that all family parties and celebrations had a personal touch.

Nowadays, Lana (Fleiszig) and Delia (Baron) have modified their grandmother's cooking to incorporate nutritious ingredients and to suit a hectic life with young children. They have skilfully adapted many of Vera's recipes by taking a faster and easier approach to cooking. They source South African products from a local delicatessen.

Most weekends, Lana's daughter, Alex, can be found perched on a kitchen stool preparing various dishes, while Maya, Delia's daughter, has perfected the art of the muffin. Lana teaches Year 5 and 6 mathematics and conducts cooking classes with her sister. They publish a weekly recipe column in the *Australian Jewish News* and have published two cookbooks. With their contemporary approach to traditional recipes, Lana and Delia continue their grandmother's heritage of innovatively cooking with their hearts and imaginations.

Africa, Zimbabwe

Chilli Beans with Mushrooms and Silverbeet

2 teaspoons olive oil

1 onion, finely chopped

2 cloves garlic, crushed

1/4 teaspoon chilli flakes

200 g (7 oz) mushrooms, chopped

1 x 720 g can mixed beans

1 x 440 g can diced tomatoes

1 x 420 ml can tomato soup

1/2 bunch silverbeet, roughly chopped

salt

pepper

Heat the oil in a saucepan and sauté the onion, garlic and chilli flakes for 5 minutes. Add the mushrooms and cook for another 5 minutes, until they start to release their juices. Add the beans, diced tomatoes and tomato soup. Gradually add the silverbeet and stir to combine. Simmer, covered, for 1½ hours, stirring occasionally.

Remove the lid and cook, uncovered, for a further 30 minutes. Season to taste. Serve with polenta or rice.

Serves 6

Peri Peri Chicken

Zimbabwe shares a border with Mozambique, which was a Portuguese colony. This dish evolved from that influence, with its piquant, hot chilli sauce used for marinating and basting.

4 baby chickens or poussins, butterflied (cut through both sides of the backbone and opened flat)

sea salt

MARINADE

1 tablespoon sambal olek (chilli paste)

1 tablespoon olive oil

juice of 1 lemon

2 teaspoons sea salt

2 teaspoons sweet paprika

2 teaspoons sugar

1/2 teaspoon Tabasco sauce

1 clove garlic, crushed

Combine the marinade ingredients and rub all over the chickens. Marinate, refrigerated, for at least 6 hours.

Preheat the oven to 250°C (500°F).

Bring the chickens to room temperature and place them in an ovenproof dish, skin side up. Reserve any marinade that remains in the dish. Sprinkle chicken with sea salt and cook for 30 minutes, basting with reserved marinade.

Serves 4

Delia and Lana Raison

African Peasant Stew

Learned from their Zimbabwean staff, this recipe takes the Raizons back to their old home, sitting beneath a tree with plates of stew. Wilted wild greens were served with it, but an Australian substitute would be silverbeet.

2 kg (4 lb) chuck steak on the bone (ask butcher to cut through the bones)

salt

pepper

2 red chillies, deseeded and finely chopped

1 tablespoon olive oil

2 large onions, finely chopped

Cut the meat into rough chunks. Season liberally with salt, pepper and a little of the chilli.

Heat the oil in a large saucepan and sauté the onions and remaining chilli until lightly golden. Add the meat in batches and cook until browned. Remove the meat from the saucepan and place in a larger, heavy-based saucepan.

Swirl the first saucepan out with ½ cup of boiling water to remove all the brown bits, and add the water to the second saucepan. Cover and cook on a low heat, turning the meat occasionally until tender, about 3 hours. A rich gravy should form at the bottom of the saucepan. If it becomes dry, add a little boiling water. Serve with polenta.

Serves 6–8

Grenadilla (Passionfruit) Tart

'We all had a lemon tree in the back garden and a grenadilla vine growing on the fence. This tart became a favourite to serve after dinner or on a lazy Sunday afternoon for tea. The Sunday afternoon tea was very "English".

PASTRY

2 cups plain flour, sifted

1 teaspoon baking powder

2 tablespoons sugar

185 g (6 oz) margarine

1 egg, lightly beaten

canola oil spray

dried beans

FILLING

3 eggs

2 egg yolks

¾ cup caster sugar

½ cup cream

juice of 2 lemons

pulp of 5 passionfruit

Preheat the oven to 190°C (375°F).

To make the pastry, mix the flour, baking powder, sugar and margarine. Add the egg and knead into a soft dough. Roll the dough to about 5 mm (¼ in) thick. (It is best to do this on plastic wrap, as it makes it easier to lift off the work bench and into the tin.) Spray a loose-bottomed muffin tin with canola oil and line it with pastry. Put baking paper over the pastry and fill with dried beans. Bake for 10 minutes.

Remove the beans and paper. Bake for a further 3 minutes, until golden. (This process is called baking blind.) Allow to cool.

Reduce the oven temperature to 150°C (300°F).

To make the filling, beat the eggs, egg yolks and sugar until thick. Add the cream and lemon juice and mix well. Strain the mixture into a jug and add the passionfruit pulp. Pour into the prepared pastry cases and bake for 20 minutes, until just set (it should be a bit wobbly in the centre when tapped).

Serves 12

Delia and Kana Raizon

Opposite (left to right) Chilli Beans with Mushrooms and Silverbeet, and African Peasant Stew

The Americas

Argentina, United States of America

THE AMERICAS ARE VAST, WITH IMMENSE VARIETY IN CLIMATE AND PRODUCE. JEWS THERE HAVE MAINTAINED THEIR OWN CULINARY REPERTOIRE, WHICH THEY BROUGHT WITH THEM FROM EASTERN EUROPE WITH THE GREAT WAVE OF IMMIGRATION IN THE EARLY PART OF THE TWENTIETH CENTURY. THE INCLUSION OF CRANBERRIES AND CRUMBLES ARE ADAPTED FROM AMERICAN CUISINE. TYPICAL JEWISH FOOD IS FOUND IN MANY DELIS IN NEW YORK, WITH SALADS, BAGELS AND DILL PICKLES THE STAR ATTRACTIONS. ARGENTINIAN CUISINE, IN CONTRAST, IS SIMILAR TO SPANISH COOKING, WITH ARGENTINA'S PROXIMITY TO THE MEXICAN BORDER ENSURING THAT AN ARRAY OF SPICES IS INCORPORATED INTO MANY DISHES.

Juanita Bekinschtein ARGENTINA

The Americas

I had a difficult childhood because Argentina was a Catholic and aggressively anti-Semitic country. I started cooking from the age of eight for my family because my mother worked with my father in their three pharmacies. I retreated into cooking: it was a haven from the struggles around me. Cooking helped me cope.

WHEN Juanita was seven years old, she discovered from her best friend, Estela, that she was Jewish. In disbelief, Juanita asked her parents whether the information was true. Her parents had disguised their Jewish identity to avoid the harsh consequences in Buenos Aires and to protect their two daughters, Juanita and Sofia. Living under a dictatorship referred to as 'the boots', Juanita recalls anti-Semitic slogans emblazoned on the streets commanding locals to 'Be patriotic. Kill a Jew.' The outspoken Juanita announced that she longed to practise Judaism, so the family started the ancient tradition of lighting candles on Friday evenings, welcoming the Sabbath. Her father, in particular, was secretly thrilled that this cultural ritual was revived in their home. He was a generous man who gave away many of the medicines from his pharmacy to the poor, so that money for household food was scant.

Juanita's father, Gregorio, was Russian while her mother, Marta, was from Argentina. Despite the harsh political environment of her childhood, Juanita remembers joyful family gatherings with cousins and aunties. Fish was frequently prepared, often gefilte fish or fried fish balls, as well as spinach or corn croquettes. Polenta and pizza were staple Argentinian foods. Juanita cherishes the memory of her mother cooking humita in a pumpkin and Chanukah empanadas – delicious savoury pastries with different fillings.

'Every year at Chanukah the "empanadas battle" took place in my house. I can still smell the glorious mixture of spices that Mum used to put in the meat – the magic, vibrant, sweet paprika and the golden cumin, the perfect marriage for a meat empanada. But empanadas are more than that. They are the soul of Argentinian cuisine and the excuse that brings friends together for a long, interesting and memorable night: a night of wine and empanadas.'

From the age of eight, Juanita adored reading and her inquisitive mind discovered Sigmund Freud at the age of twelve. As a teenager, she attended a Jewish social club, Hebraica, often skating and dancing with her cousins. She loved to accompany her mother to the feria – the local street market with stalls laden with meat, fish and vegetables.

'When I was a little girl, people used to buy all their fresh ingredients in the ferias. You walked along a particular street that was chosen for the feria that day, between stalls with hanging chickens all feathered, fish so big that some of them took up the whole length of the counter. The fishmonger didn't wear proper shoes but some kind of wooden clogs that amazed me. The meat wasn't refrigerated – it sat on marble slabs to keep it cool. Mum and I always came back from the feria with a beautiful pumpkin and with lots of lollies that the fishmonger gave me just to keep me quiet. Those amazing days of my childhood are gone forever, but the colourful and vibrant memories are always in my mind.'

The colours and textures of the fresh market produce ignited her curiosity about cooking. Her mother explained the basic principles – how to combine spices and the rudimentary methods of preparation – and soon Juanita was cooking for her entire family while her parents worked as pharmacists.

'Mother said, "Open the cabinet and do whatever you want. Just mix things".' Juanita would prepare fried fish fillets and salads for her sister when she returned from school, picking tiny buds from their flower bed to decorate the plates. 'I love abundance and refinement. I wouldn't have a table full of food without thinking of how the colours blend. One colour exalts the other. I would never make two dishes that clash.'

From the age of seven, Juanita ironed while perched on a little stool, despite repeatedly burning her hands. Her beautiful aunt, Negra, with her black, curly hair, confided in her about her lover and unhappy marriage while little Juanita, a responsible and imaginative girl, sat on a biscuit tin, listening. 'Even though I was small, I was born old.' Her other aunt, Rosa, taught little Juanita how to make kreplach – traditional meat dumplings.

Juanita's family rented a typical, old Argentinian house with a long corridor, and their landlady, who was openly anti-Semitic, lived in the rear of the property. When Juanita and her sister were home alone, she would kick the door and scream abuse. The young girls lived in fear. Sometimes, Juanita found refuge in Estela's opulent home.

Juanita's maternal grandfather was a chazzan (a cantor) in the local synagogue and she recalls him praying and singing hypnotic tunes. Her paternal grandfather took Juanita to Ingmar Bergman films as a teenager, as one needed to be accompanied by an adult. He used to tell her joyful stories and was complicit in her strong desire to escape from her oppressive surroundings. Their special bond and outings are a precious memory.

For the Sabbath, Juanita would help her mother prepare chicken casserole with potatoes, omelettes and croquettes. A type of crème caramel was presented for dessert. Gnocchi was a regular feature that was traditionally served on the twenty-eighth day of every month, with money left under the plate for good luck.

Since dancing is a significant feature of Argentinian life, Juanita started learning ballet and drama, and became a drama teacher, while attending endless rehearsals at night. At twenty-three, she married Joseph, and his mother Herminia became an important culinary influence, sharing what she had learned from classes given by renowned international chefs. For Juanita she had 'gold in her hands'. Juanita took cooking lessons from a high-society Buenos Aires widow, Chocha, whose flourless chocolate roulade is now part of Juanita's repertoire. Like her mother, Juanita takes great culinary pleasure in the creativity of baking and decorating cakes.

Juanita was reluctant to leave Argentina with her two children – Debra and Diego – as she enjoyed the cosmopolitan life of Buenos Aires and performing in the theatre. The family decided, however, that Australia might provide a brighter future and more opportunities. Joseph was an electromechanical engineer with skills that were sought by immigration. After a period of time in Sydney, they settled in Melbourne. Food became a way for Juanita to adapt to her new environment. 'I have a passion for food. It keeps the flame going between two people. It is my great love. Since childhood, cooking has always been a kind of path to engage with people, a way of communicating.' Now Juanita loves cooking with her two beloved grandchildren, Ellie and Jordan.

Juanita Bekinschtein

Chanukah Empanadas

Chanukah, the festival of lights, is when Jews commemorate the little jug of oil that miraculously burned for eight days. These fried pastries are traditionally eaten during the festival.

FILLING

3 tablespoons olive oil

1 large red onion, finely chopped

1 large red capsicum, finely chopped

½ teaspoon sweet paprika

¼ teaspoon ground cumin

¼ teaspoon ground black pepper

250 g (9 oz) minced beef (not diet mince)

1 teaspoon salt

½ cup water

1 heaped tablespoon plain flour

2 hard-boiled eggs, finely chopped

DOUGH

125 g (4 oz) plain flour

½ teaspoon salt

30 g (1 oz) butter

2–3 tablespoons water

sunflower oil for frying

To make the filling, heat the oil in a deep frying pan on a high heat. Add the onion, lower the heat to medium and stir regularly. When the onion is transparent, add the capsicum. Stir continuously. When the capsicum softens, add the paprika, cumin and pepper, and continue stirring. Add the beef and brown. Add the salt and water and cook for a further 10 minutes on a low heat. Stir in the flour. Add the eggs. Set aside to cool.

To make the dough, sift the flour and the salt into a bowl. Rub in the butter until the mixture resembles breadcrumbs. Add the water and knead thoroughly on a floured board to form a very smooth dough. Cover it with a tea towel and allow to rest for 10 minutes. (If the weather is hot, chill the pastry, otherwise it will be difficult to roll.) Divide the dough into about eight pieces. Dust each piece with flour and, with a rolling pin, roll into a circle about 1 cm (½ in) thick. Put 1 teaspoon of the filling in the middle, fold the dough over and close firmly at the edges. With a fork go over the edges to make a pattern, making sure they are securely closed.

Heat the oil in a wok or large saucepan and deep-fry the empanadas until golden brown.

Makes 8

The Americas, Argentina

Humita in a Pumpkin

'Humita' is Spanish for 'corn' or 'maize'. Corn is an integral part of the Argentinian diet.
The pumpkin in this recipe can be prepared in advance.

1 jap or grey pumpkin for presentation

5 cobs of corn, with husks

1 jap or grey pumpkin, cut into chunks

olive oil

2 red onions, finely chopped

1 large yellow capsicum, finely chopped

1 large red capsicum, finely chopped

2 tablespoons ground cumin

2 tablespoons sweet paprika

2 tablespoons Madras curry powder

1 teaspoon salt

1 teaspoon ground black pepper

2 x 440 g cans corn kernels

3 tablespoons polenta

The size of the pumpkin for presentation depends on the number of people you are serving. This pumpkin is not for eating, and the dish can be served without it. To prepare this pumpkin, the day before serving, preheat the oven to 180°C (350°F) and bake the whole pumpkin, with skin, for 1 hour, until softened but retaining its shape. When it is soft, cut off the top part to make a lid and scoop out the flesh and seeds. Refrigerate. It will keep up to three days.

Remove and reserve the corn husks. Put the corn in a saucepan of boiling water and cook, covered, for 10 minutes, until tender. When cool, separate the kernels and reserve two of the cobs for garnishing.

Cook the pumpkin pieces in a saucepan of boiling water for 10 minutes, until tender but not too mushy. Be sure to cook only one layer at a time, so that the pumpkin cooks evenly.

Preheat the oven to 170°C (340°F).

Heat the oil in a saucepan on a high heat. Add the onions, stirring until soft and transparent. Add the capsicums and cook until softened. Add the cumin, paprika, curry powder, salt and pepper and stir. Add the fresh corn kernels and the pumpkin pieces to the saucepan, then the canned corn with its juices, and the polenta. Cook, stirring continuously, for 15 minutes, until the mixture thickens.

Transfer the mixture to an ovenproof dish and cook in the oven for 20 minutes or until solid.

For a breathtaking presentation, remove the pumpkin shell from the refrigerator and warm in the oven for 15 minutes. Fill the shell with the hot mixture, and return the lid to its place. Bake for another 20 minutes. Serve hot, garnished with the cobs of corn.

Serves 12–14

Polenta Gnocchi with a Rich Tomato Sauce and Fresh Herbs

'Of course I am not Italian but being Argentinian is close enough. Doña Helena Tebano was the mum of my best friend, Carmencita. They used to cook gnocchi twice a week. I would hold my breath waiting for Carmencita to ask me for dinner. Doña Helena taught me her cooking secrets, but my long love affair with the gnocchi began later in life when I started making them. The Tebano family was part of my treasured life in Argentina, and is part of my life today whenever I make those golden yellow and red circles in Doña Helena's memory.'

TOMATO SAUCE

4 tablespoons olive oil

2 large red onions, finely chopped

1 large red capsicum, finely chopped

3 tablespoons sweet paprika

1 teaspoon salt

$\frac{1}{2}$ teaspoon ground black pepper

2 cloves garlic, minced

4 x 440 g cans tomatoes, finely chopped

$\frac{1}{2}$ cup flat-leaf parsley, finely chopped

GNOCCHI

1 litre (2 pints) full-cream milk

2 teaspoons salt

1 teaspoon ground black pepper

125 g (4 oz) butter, softened

$\frac{1}{2}$ teaspoon ground nutmeg

250 g (9 oz) polenta

$\frac{1}{2}$ cup freshly grated Parmesan

knob of butter

$\frac{1}{2}$ cup freshly grated mozzarella

In a large saucepan heat the oil on a high heat and sauté the onions until transparent. Add the capsicum and, when softened, add the paprika, salt, pepper, garlic, tomatoes and parsley. Stir until well combined. Cook on a high heat for 6–7 minutes, then on a low heat for 1 hour, uncovered, until thick and rich in colour. Set aside.

Preheat the oven to 250°C (500°F).

To make the gnocchi, pour the milk into a large saucepan and bring to the boil. Add the salt, pepper, butter and nutmeg, and stir. Lower the heat. Sprinkle the polenta into the milk while continuously stirring. Add the Parmesan and cook for 1 minute, until it thickens to a porridge-like consistency.

Grease a working surface. Marble or granite is ideal, but a tray lined with baking paper is a good substitute. Spread the hot polenta with a knife or spatula to your preferred thickness of gnocchi. Allow to cool. Cut the polenta into shapes with a small biscuit cutter, about 10 cm (4 in) in diameter.

Spread some tomato sauce on the bottom of a shallow baking dish. Arrange the gnocchi in a pyramid configuration, topped with a small knob of butter. Bake for 10 minutes. Lower the oven temperature to 160°C (320°F). Spoon the remaining sauce over the gnocchi and top with mozzarella. Bake until the cheese melts. Serve immediately.

Serves 8–10

Apple Doughnuts

Buñuelos

Buñuelos – Argentinian doughnuts – are a 'must' at any Argentinian Chanukah table.
A banana can be substituted if preferred to apples.

350 g (12½ oz) plain flour
pinch of salt
3 tablespoons sugar
1 teaspoon baking powder
1½ cups full-cream milk
3 eggs, separated
1 large red apple
sunflower oil for frying

Mix the flour, salt, sugar, baking powder, milk and egg yolks until well combined. Beat the egg whites until they form soft peaks, then add them to the mixture.

Roughly chop the apple and add to the batter.

Heat the oil in a wok or large saucepan. Spoon tablespoons of the batter into the oil and fry until golden. Turn to brown evenly. Serve hot.

Makes 20

Flourless Chocolate Roulade

Arrollado de Chocolate Sin Harina

For four years, Juanita learned Chocha's elaborate cooking and distinctly remembers the flourless chocolate roulade, served with a rich chocolate sauce or fruit coulis.

8 large eggs, separated
250 g (9 oz) caster sugar
250 g (9 oz) dark cooking chocolate
300 ml (11 fl oz) thickened cream
200 g (7 oz) icing sugar
600 g canned dark plums, drained

Preheat the oven to 170°C (340°F).

Beat the egg whites until they form soft peaks, and set aside. Beat the yolks with the sugar until blended and pale.

Melt the chocolate in a double boiler or a small saucepan placed in a larger saucepan containing boiling water. Add the chocolate to the egg yolks and mix until combined. Do not overmix. Fold in the whites.

Line a 40 cm x 30 cm (16 in x 12 in) tin with baking paper, and spread mixture into it. Bake for 20 minutes, until set. Remove the tin from the oven and test the cake with a toothpick. If it comes out clean, the cake is set. If not, bake for a further 10–15 minutes. Remove from the oven and cover with a damp tea towel, allowing it to cool.

Beat the cream with the icing sugar until thick. When the cake has cooled, spread the cream over the top and place plum pieces evenly over it. From the wider end, roll the log, using the baking paper as the rolling tool. Mark the slices with a knife at regular intervals. Refrigerate for 2 hours, until set.

Serve at room temperature or frozen with a warm chocolate sauce or fruit coulis. Decorate with chunky pieces of chocolate and fresh camellia leaves.

Serves 12–14

Rivkah Groner USA

My mother allowed her daughters to freely experiment with cooking. *From the age of ten, I was baking an apple cake for Shabbat and soon after I prepared a light, milchig supper of salmon patties as well as macaroni and cheese. I could easily follow recipes and always enjoyed cooking.*

BORN in Worcester, Massachusetts in 1964, Rivkah grew up in a family of four sisters and one brother. Her father, Yisroel, is a rabbi from a small Polish village, Dokszycz, while her Russian mother, Miriam, migrated after the war, having struggled in harsh conditions in Siberia as a teenager. Rivkah's paternal grandfather, Yochonon, was a shochet – a ritual slaughterer for meat – who travelled to New York in 1930 seeking work, following his brothers who had already settled there. After a few years, he sent for his wife, Zeesy, and their four children to join him in 1934.

Rivkah's maternal grandfather, Dovber Paltiel, was in the army during the war while her mother and two brothers lived in various orphanages. In 1945, they travelled with a Lubavitch family to a displaced persons camp in Austria, then settled in Paris for a couple of years. Dovber, a scholar and teacher, had remarried a seamstress after the loss of his first wife and they moved to New York in the late 1940s. In the early 1950s, Rivkah's father, Yisroel, completed his rabbinical studies. At the age of twenty, he was sent by Rebbe Menachem Schneerson, the spiritual leader of the Lubavitch community, to Worcester, a four-hour drive from New York.

Previously, Rabbi Yosef Schneerson had been instrumental in setting up orthodox schools and synagogues in the United States. The Lubavitcher movement is known as Chabad – an acronym for wisdom, understanding and knowledge. As the youngest child, Yisroel found it difficult to leave his parents but he was instructed to fulfil his duties of revitalising Jewish communities. His arranged marriage to Miriam took place in 1955. Soon after, they welcomed Zeesy, Rishe, Rivkah, Etty and Yossy.

There were no kosher restaurants in the small town of Worcester. Every month, various products, often frozen, were delivered from New York by truck. Fortunately, the local bakery sold some kosher bread. When Rivkah visited New York at the age of fifteen, she was struck by 'the availability of kosher products and food, especially ice-cream'.

For the Sabbath meal Rivkah's mother prepared traditional feasts comprising gefilte fish, chicken soup, roast chicken and lokshen kugel. Suspicious of new utensils such as the food processor, she chopped eggs and liver with a mezzaluna – a curved, double-handled blade in the shape of a half-moon.

Rivkah recalls the strong aroma of boiling liver – a necessary process for kashrut – filling the home with a pungent smell. Rivkah became intrigued by the American food served by her neighbours, the chocolate milk and hot dogs. Before Rivkah's oldest sister, Rishe, married, she spent an entire summer following their mother, avidly transcribing recipes. An adventurous cook, Rivkah enjoyed experimenting in the kitchen from a young age. Even her brother makes a fabulous cholent.

Every Passover, Rivkah and her extended family united for a delicious feast, when the cousins would vehemently argue as to whose mother was a better cook. Rivkah's mother and her sisters would cook together, preparing potato kugel, chicken soup, apple sauce and Passover cakes. Meanwhile, nine children sat on the porch with a large bin, busily peeling bags of potatoes.

Rivkah attended The Yeshivah, a small Jewish day school in Worcester, but moved to live with Rishe in New York for the last two years of high school. Keen to attend a more challenging school, she began studies at Beth Rivkah. When her sister and brother-in-law went out for dinner she was the babysitter, eagerly looking forward to the food parcels they would bring home from various kosher restaurants, particularly Chinese. Rivkah marvelled at Kosher Delight – an American fast food chain. Her other sister, Zeesy, lived in Skokie, Chicago, where Rivkah stayed over the summer to work at a Jewish day camp.

The Lubavitcher headquarters were located in Crown Heights, Brooklyn, in an old mansion that contained the Yeshivah, synagogue, library and Rebbe's offices as well as an educational centre. Rivkah completed her teaching degree nearby. Introduced to her husband by an acquaintance in New York, Rivkah married Chaim, a rabbi, in December 1982. Six months later, Chaim was offered a position at the Kollel in Melbourne, where married men undertake a two-year program of tertiary studies after rabbinical ordination. On the day before their departure, Rivkah met the Holy Rebbe as he was walking towards afternoon prayer. He stopped and uttered, 'Besuros tovos-fuhr gezunter heit' – 'We should hear good news, have a safe journey', in Yiddish and Hebrew. Uncertain about travelling, Rivkah immediately felt reassured of their plans, as if divine providence brought her family to Australia with the Rebbe's blessing.

Chaim studied all day and presented public lessons in the evening. Within weeks of their arrival, Rivkah discovered she was pregnant. She was teaching at Beth Rivkah Ladies' College and slowly adjusting to the quiet life in Australia, 'where nothing was open on Sundays'. Even phoning family at home was expensive and complicated. Rivkah longed for the pulsating lifestyle of New York. 'I felt like I had come to the moon, so far away. I missed my family and couldn't understand the accent. Butcher shops had meat in different names and the supply was limited in those days.' After two years in Australia, Rivkah and Chaim were in a quandary as to whether they should remain, so they sought the Rebbe's advice. He suggested that they seek the opinion of close friends. As a result, their fate was sealed and they stayed in Melbourne. When Rivkah had her children she finally appreciated the pace in Australia.

Rivkah Groner

Before Rivkah married, her sister Zeesy presented her with a box full of blank cards. Rivkah diligently transcribed the family recipes such as Zeesy's tasty pea soup. To this day, she frequently consults this box, which is now brimming with fabulous recipes. All of Rivkah's siblings have signature dishes: Rishe prepares a tasty sweet potato pie and Etty cooks a savoury zucchini kugel. Her Californian neighbour, Natalie, has passed on her recipe for apple cranberry dessert and Debbie from Atlanta, who works at Solomon's butcher, has handed over her recipe for pickled brisket. Many of her American friends share their recipes in this close-knit community, preferring nutritious, wholesome food that is straightforward to prepare.

Rivkah enjoys adapting dishes from her library of cookbooks, ensuring a healthy cuisine for her nine children, some of whom adore cooking. Mushka is known as the 'salad queen' but she has also been baking challah and kneidlach from a young age, partly inspired by her mother's cooking and by learning home economics at school. Chana, twenty, cooks meat; Yosl, seventeen, fries chicken schnitzels on Friday afternoons; and Rivkah's husband is adept at preparing gefilte fish. Together, 'they enjoy making people happy and satisfied. For Jewish people, every special event is around food; every Yom Tov has its own special dishes.' Rivkah maintains the Jewish traditions in her orthodox home with latkes (potato pancakes) for Chanukah, cheesecake for Shavuot and hamantashen for Purim. The result is a welcoming, hearty Jewish cuisine enjoyed by the many guests that flock to Rivkah's home.

Zeesy's Pea Soup

1½ cups green split peas
½ cup yellow split peas
10 cups water
1 onion, finely chopped
2 carrots, grated
2 stalks celery, finely chopped
2½ teaspoons salt
2 teaspoons dried parsley
3 potatoes, finely chopped

Bring all the ingredients to the boil, except the potatoes. Cook on a low heat for 2½ hours. Add the potatoes and cook for a further 30 minutes.

Serves 4–6

Debbie's Pickled Brisket

This dish is typically served on the Sabbath.

1–1.5 kg (2–3 lb) pickled brisket, vacuum-packed from butcher
5 peppercorns
2 cloves garlic
3 bay leaves
½ cup brown sugar
¼ cup vinegar

Place all the ingredients in a large saucepan and bring to the boil. Simmer, covered, on a low heat for 1 hour per kilogram (2 lb). Remove the brisket and slice when cool.

Serves 6–8

Etty's Zucchini Kugel

6 eggs, beaten

6 zucchini, grated

1 large onion, grated

½ cup vegetable oil

2 teaspoons salt

½ teaspoon ground black pepper

1 cup self-raising flour

Preheat the oven to 180°C (350°F).

Combine the eggs with the grated zucchini and onion. Add the remaining ingredients and mix well.

Line a baking dish with baking paper and pour the mixture into the dish. Bake, uncovered, for 45–55 minutes. Serve hot.

Serves 4–6

Rishe's Sweet Potato Pie

PIE CRUST

⅓ cup margarine

1 cup self-raising flour

2 tablespoons cold water

FILLING

2 sweet potatoes, cut into chunks

1 egg white

2 teaspoons ground cinnamon

½ cup brown sugar

To make the pie crust, mix the margarine into the flour in a bowl with a pastry blender or with two butter knives. Continue mixing until it is the consistency of small peas. Sprinkle with cold water. Mix with a fork or a pastry blender until the mixture forms a ball. Dust your hands with flour and roll out the dough onto a floured surface into a circle about 1 cm (½ in) thick. Press into a 22 cm (9 in) round pie dish.

Preheat the oven to 180°C (350°F).

To make the filling, in a saucepan cover the sweet potatoes with water and bring to the boil. Simmer on a medium heat for about 10 minutes, until soft. Mash the sweet potatoes with a potato masher until smooth, then mix with the egg white, cinnamon and sugar. Spoon the mixture into the pie crust and bake for 1 hour. Serve hot.

Serves 8

Rivkah Groner

Natalie's Apple Cranberry Dessert

Cranberries and apples in a sublime combination.

5 granny smith apples, peeled and chopped

1 x 440 g can cranberries

1 cup brown sugar

½ cup margarine

1 cup plain flour or oats

Preheat the oven to 180°C (350°F).

Place the apples in a greased 23 cm (9 in) square baking tin. Pour the cranberries over the apples and mix gently. Mix the sugar, margarine and flour, and spoon over the fruit.

Bake for 30–40 minutes, until the apples are soft. Serve with ice-cream.

Serves 8

Glossary

Afrikaans	A language derived from Dutch that is spoken in South Africa
Ashkenazi Jews	Jews whose culture and origin is that of Eastern Europe and Russia
brisket	A cut of beef taken from behind the foreshank of a cow
bumbu	Indonesian curry paste
candlenuts	Hard-shelled nuts with a high oil content, named for their use in making simple candles, used in Indonesian cooking
challah	Plaited egg loaf eaten on the Sabbath
Chanukah	(Also spelled 'Hanukkah') Jewish festival of lights, in which fried foods are traditionally eaten
cholent	A tasty stew that includes meat, potatoes, beans and rice or barley in a variety of combinations. It is commonly served on the Sabbath day during the noon meal. Every culture has its own version and the spelling is sometimes 'chulent'.
garam masala	An aromatic Indian spice mix available in Asian stores or food departments
gefilte fish	Polish fish balls, served cold
kashrut	Jewish dietary observances defining which foods are kosher, or permissible for consumption by Jews
kencur	(Lesser galangal) rhizome with a flavour between pepper and ginger, which is available at Asian grocery stores
kiddushim	Appetisers served after the synagogue service
kneidlach	Soup dumplings made from matzo meal and eggs
kreplach	Traditional meat dumplings
kugel	(Yiddish for 'ball') A Jewish pudding made with vegetables or sometimes noodles or fruit
lokshen	Egg noodles, served in soup
Lubavitch	An active global Jewish network instructed by His Majesty King Messiah with the purpose of promulgating Jewish philosophy and guidance (adjective: Lubavitcher)
matzo	A crisp unleavened biscuit eaten on Passover
matzo meal	Crumbed matzo used to make matzo balls

milchig	Food containing dairy
parve	Food containing no meat or milk derivatives which may be used at either meat or milk meals, e.g. fish, eggs, juice, fruits and vegetables
Pesach	A major Jewish festival (also called Passover) commemorating the liberation of the Israelites from Egyptian slavery, at which matzo – unleavened bread – is eaten
pilau	Rice dish
Purim	A Jewish festive holiday celebrating the rescue of the Jews from a plot to destroy them. Fancy dress and hamantashen (sweet biscuits) are hallmarks of the celebration.
Rebbe	The spiritual leader of the Lubavitch Jews
Rosh Hashanah	Jewish New Year
Sabbath	The Jewish holy day, which lasts from sunset on Friday to sunset on Saturday (in Hebrew, Shabbat)
seder	The ritual gathering and meal that takes place on the first two nights of Pesach
Sephardi Jews	Jews whose culture and origin is that of countries bordering the Mediterranean Sea, the Middle East, Asia and Africa
sukkah	A temporary house made with three walls and a roof of palm fronds which Jewish people live in for seven days to recall biblical times when Jews did not have a homeland or a permanent dwelling
Sukkot	A Jewish festival during which Jews build and inhabit a temporary dwelling (sukkah) for seven days to commemorate the forty-year period in history when Jews wandered in the desert before arriving at their homeland
tamarind juice	Juice reconstituted from the pulp of the tamarind fruit
Torah	The five books of the bible (the Old Testament)
toshi koshi soba	Long Japanese noodles made from a combination of buckwheat and wheat flour
ulpan	A study trip to Israel
Yeshivah	A place where orthodox Jews study the Torah and Jewish law
Yom Kippur	Jewish day of atonement, during which observant Jews fast
Yom Tov	Jewish holy day

Glossary

Index

A
African Peasant Stew 157
appetisers
  Fish Patties 92
  Stuffed Vine Leaves 83
  Zucchini Antipasto 47
  see also dips
apples
  Apple Doughnuts 168
  Natalie's Apple Cranberry Dessert
    176
Arrollado de Chocolate Sin Harina
  168
artichokes
  Stuffed Artichokes 70
Asparagus with Eggs and Vinaigrette
  29
Atzil, Miriam 110–18

B
Baba Ghanoush 69
Barak, Yaffa 65–76
Batinjan Mlabbal 83
beans
  Chilli Beans with Mushrooms and
    Silverbeet 155
  Green Lobio 6
  Ice-cream with Adzuki Beans 109
  Red Lobio Salad 6
béchamel sauce 43
beef
  African Peasant Stew 157
  Beef Rendang 102
  Beef in Teriyaki Sauce 108
  Chanukah Empanadas 164
  Debbie's Pickled Brisket 173
  Moroccan Couscous with Beef
    and Vegetables 141
  Scotch Fillet with Green Pea
    Sauce 45
  Steakhouse Marinade 148
  Vietnamese Beef Salad 126
beetroot
  Beetroot Salad 5
  Beetroot Soup (Borscht) 20
  Beetroot Stew 64
Bekinschtein, Juanita 160–8
Birner, Raquella 78–84

biscuits
  South African Rusks 149
  Strudel Biscuits (Rugelach) 16
  Sweet Biscuits (Kichel) 149
Boolkes 151
Borscht 20
breads
  Flat Bread with Cumin Seeds 61
  Indian Bread (Chapatti) 89
Bukharan Delight 118
buns
  Cinnamon Buns (Boolkes) 151
Buñuelos 168

C
Cabbage Rolls 23
cakes
  Chocolate Cake 30
  Concorde Cake 32
  Dundee Cake 56
  Flourless Chocolate Roulade 168
  Hazelnut Meringue Chocolate
    Mousse Cake 76
  Poppyseed Cake 39
  Semolina Cake (Safra) 134
Caledonian Cream 54
Carrot Halwa 93
casseroles and stews
  African Peasant Stew 157
  Beetroot Stew 64
  Lamb Casserole with Prunes 73
  Lamb Stew (Chanahi) 8
  Red Wine Chicken Casserole
    (Coq au Vin) 30
Cauliflower and Aniseed (Fennel)
  Salad 61
Caviglia, Perla 40–8
Cha Gio Chiên 123
Chanahi 8
Chanukah Empanadas 164
Chapatti 89
chicken
  Chicken with Chickpeas 133
  Chicken in a Mixed Nut Sauce
    (Satsivi) 8
  Chicken Paprika 39
  Chicken Soup 12
  Chicken Tagine 141

Chicken and Vegetable Soup 36
  Curried Chicken, Javanese Style
    100
  Italian Meat Loaf 45
  Peri Peri Chicken 155
  Red Chicken Curry 93
  Red Wine Chicken Casserole
    (Coq au Vin) 30
  Roast Chicken 15
  stock 125
  Winter Warmer Chicken 115
chickpeas
  Chicken with Chickpeas 133
  Chickpeas with Sesame Seed
    Paste (Hummus Bi-Tahini) 81
  Sweet and Sour Chickpeas 90
Chilli Beans with Mushrooms and
  Silverbeet 155
chocolate
  Chocolate Cake 30
  cream 32
  Flourless Chocolate Roulade
    168
  ganache 30
  Hazelnut Meringue Chocolate
    Mousse Cake 76
  mousse 76
Cholent in a Bag (Oshi-Sabo) 116
Chubiz 61
Chuoi Nep Chung Nuoc Dua 126
Cinnamon Buns (Boolkes) 151
coconut
  Coconut Rice 92
  Sticky Coconut Rice Pudding
    126
Concia 47
Concorde Cake 32
Cooked Salad (Madbucha) 69
Coq au Vin 30
Coriander Carp 115
corn
  Humita in a Pumpkin 165
couscous
  Moroccan Couscous with Beef
    and Vegetables 141
cranberries
  Natalie's Apple Cranberry Dessert
    176

creams
    Caledonian 54
    chocolate 32
    pâtissière 32
Csirke Paprikás 39
Cucumber, Tomato and Onion
    Salad 89
curry
    Curried Chicken, Javanese
        Style 100
    Red Chicken Curry 93

D
Debbie's Pickled Brisket 173
desserts
    Bukharan Delight 118
    Caledonian Cream 54
    Ice-cream with Adzuki Beans 109
    Malva Pudding 148
    Natalie's Apple Cranberry
        Dessert 176
    Non-dairy Tiramisu 134
    Peaches with Lemon 48
    Pears in Red Wine 47
    Rishe's Sweet Potato Pie 175
    Sticky Coconut Rice Pudding 126
    Strawberries with Balsamic
        Vinegar 48
    Sweet Dumplings (Vareniki) 24
    see also cakes; tarts
dips
    Chickpeas with Sesame Seed
        Paste (Hummus Bi-Tahini) 81
    Cooked Salad (Madbucha) 69
    Eggplant Salad 83
    Eggplant Salad with Mayonnaise
        (Baba Ghanoush) 69
    Eggplant Salad with Red
        Capsicums 72
doughnuts
    Apple Doughnuts 168
dumplings
    Feather-light Matzo Balls
        (Kneidlach) 12
    kibba 64
    Savoury Dumplings (Pirochki) 23
    Sweet Dumplings (Vareniki) 24
Dundee Cake 56

E
Edulmuth, June 143–51
eggplant
    Eggplant Salad 83

Eggplant Salad with Mayonnaise
    (Baba Ghanoush) 69
Eggplant Salad with Red
    Capsicums 72
Ratatouille 139
eggs
    Scotch Eggs 54
Elijah, Hannah 86–93
empanadas
    Chanukah Empanadas 164
Etty's Zucchini Kugel 175

F
Farfalle with Vodka 44
Feather-light Matzo Balls 12
fennel
    Cauliflower and Aniseed (Fennel)
        Salad 61
fish
    Coriander Carp 115
    Fish Balls (Gefilte Fish) 14
    Fish in Ginger Soy Sauce 108
    Fish Patties 92
    Fish in Tahini Sauce 84
    Moroccan Fish Balls 75
    Moroccan Spicy Fish 139
    Roll-your-own Sushi (Temaki
        Sushi) 106
    Spicy Fish (Sambal Goreng
        Ikan) 99
    stock 14
    Tweed Kettle 53
Flat Bread with Cumin Seeds 61
Flourless Chocolate Roulade 168
Fragole con Aceto Balsamico 48
Fruit Tart 32
Fusilli with Fresh Tomato Sauce 44

G
gado-gado
    Indonesian Salad (Lotek) 98
Gefilte Fish 14
Georgian Lamb Soup (Kharcho) 5
gnocchi
    Polenta Gnocchi with a Rich
        Tomato Sauce and Fresh
        Herbs 166
Goi Bo 126
Goldschlager, Dina 128–34
Gombas Rizs 37
granola
    Low-fat Granola 146
Green Bean Dish (Green Lobio) 6

green pea sauce 45
Greenfield, Miriam 119–26
Grenadilla (Passionfruit) Tart 157
Groner, Rivkah 169–76

H
Hazelnut Meringue Chocolate
    Mousse Cake 76
Hirsh, Shirley 9–16
Humita in a Pumpkin 165
hummus
    Chickpeas with Sesame Seed
        Paste (Hummus Bi-Tahini) 81

I
Ice-cream with Adzuki Beans 109
Indian Bread (Chapatti) 89
Indonesian Salad (Lotek) 98
Italian Meat Loaf 45

J
Jawary, Nita 58–64
Jewish Spring Rolls (Piroshki) 14

K
Keinan, Eva 136–41
Kharcho 5
Khazam, Bram 95–102
kibba 64
Kibba Shuandr 64
Kichel 149
Kneidlach 12
Kojia, Luba 2–8
kugel
    Etty's Zucchini Kugel 175

L
lamb
    Cholent in a Bag (Oshi-Sabo) 116
    Georgian Lamb Soup (Kharcho) 5
    kibba 64
    Lamb Casserole with Prunes 73
    Lamb Stew (Chanahi) 8
    Rice with Lamb and Pineapple
        (Plof) 24
    Scotch Broth 53
Lavz 118
Lentil and Rice Pilaf (Mjadrah) 84
lobio
    Bean Salad (Red Lobio Salad) 6
    Green Bean Dish (Green Lobio) 6
Lotek 98
Low-fat Granola 146

M
Madbucha 69
Mákos Torta 39
Malva Pudding 148
marinade
    Steakhouse Marinade 148
matzo balls
    Feather-light Matzo Balls
        (Kneidlach) 12
meat loaf
    Italian Meat Loaf 45
Meatballs 133
meringue 32, 76
Mishi Warak Enab 83
Mjadrah 84
Moroccan Couscous with Beef and
    Vegetables 141
Moroccan Fish Balls 75
Moroccan Spicy Fish 139
mousse, chocolate 76
mushrooms
    Chilli Beans with Mushrooms and
        Silverbeet 155
    Mushrooms and Rice 37

N
Natalie's Apple Cranberry
    Dessert 176
Non-dairy Tiramisu 134
noodles
    Vietnamese Rice Noodle Soup
        (Pho Ga) 125
nuoc mam 123
nuts
    Bukharan Delight (Lavz) 118
    Chicken in a Mixed Nut Sauce
        (Satsivi) 8
    Hazelnut Meringue Chocolate
        Mousse Cake 76

O
onions
    Cucumber, Tomato and Onion
        Salad 89
    Onion Rice 62
Oshi-Sabo 116

P
passionfruit
    Grenadilla (Passionfruit) Tart 157
pasta
    Farfalle with Vodka 44
    Fusilli with Fresh Tomato Sauce 44

Penne with Béchamel Sauce 43
pastry
    shortcrust 32
    strudel 16
patties
    Fish Patties 92
Pea Pilau 90
Peaches with Lemon 48
Pears in Red Wine 47
peas
    green pea sauce 45
    Pea Pilau 90
    Zeesy's Pea Soup 173
Penne with Béchamel Sauce 43
Pere al Vino Rosso 47
Peri Peri Chicken 155
Pesche al Limone 48
Pho Ga 125
Pickled Vegetables 131
pies
    Rishe's Sweet Potato Pie 175
pilaf
    Lentil and Rice Pilaf
        (Mjadrah) 84
    Pea Pilau 90
pineapple
    Rice with Lamb and Pineapple
        (Plof) 24
Pirochki 23
Piroshki 14
Plof 24
Polenta Gnocchi with a Rich Tomato
    Sauce and Fresh Herbs 166
Polpettone di Pollo 45
Pomodori con Riso 43
Poppyseed Cake 39
Potage aux Epinards 29
potatoes
    Russian Potato Salad 20

R
Raizon, Delia and Lana 152–7
Ratatouille 139
Red Chicken Curry 93
Red Wine Chicken Casserole (Coq
    au Vin) 30
Reine de Saba 30
Ress, Suzanne 26–32
rice
    Cholent in a Bag (Oshi-Sabo) 116
    Coconut Rice 92
    Lentil and Rice Pilaf (Mjadrah) 84
    Mushrooms and Rice 37

Onion Rice 62
Pea Pilau 90
Rice with Lamb and Pineapple
    (Plof) 24
Rice Salad 131
Sticky Coconut Rice Pudding 126
for sushi 106
Tomatoes Stuffed with Rice 43
Rishe's Sweet Potato Pie 175
Roast Chicken 15
Roasted Vegetable Salad 72
Roitman, Susie 17–24
Roll-your-own Sushi 106
Rugelach 16
rusks
    South African Rusks 149
Russian Potato Salad 20
Ryan, Yoko 103–9

S
Safra 134
salads
    Bean Salad (Red Lobio Salad) 6
    Beetroot Salad 5
    Cauliflower and Aniseed (Fennel)
        Salad 61
    Cucumber, Tomato and Onion
        Salad 89
    Indonesian Salad (Lotek) 98
    Rice Salad 131
    Roasted Vegetable Salad 72
    Russian Potato Salad 20
    Strawberry Fields Salad 146
    Tabbouleh 81
    Vietnamese Beef Salad 126
    see also dips
Samak Bi-Taratur 84
Sambal Goreng Ikan 99
Satsivi 8
sauces
    nuoc mam 123
    tahini 84
Savoury Dumplings (Pirochki) 23
Scotch Broth 53
Scotch Eggs 54
Scotch Fillet with Green Pea
    Sauce 45
Semolina Cake (Safra) 134
Shapiro, Hazel 49–56
shortcrust pastry 32
silverbeet
    Chilli Beans with Mushrooms and
        Silverbeet 155

soups
    Beetroot Soup (Borscht) 20
    Chicken Soup 12
    Chicken and Vegetable Soup 36
    Georgian Lamb Soup (Kharcho) 5
    Scotch Broth 53
    Spinach Soup 29
    Vietnamese Rice Noodle Soup
      (Pho Ga) 125
    Zeesy's Pea Soup 173
South African Rusks 149
Spenot 37
Spezzatino con Piselli 45
Spicy Fish (Sambal Goreng Ikan) 99
spinach
    Spinach (Spenot) 37
    Spinach Soup 29
spring rolls
    Jewish Spring Rolls (Piroshki) 14
    Vietnamese Spring Rolls 123
Steakhouse Marinade 148
stews *see* casseroles and stews
Sticky Coconut Rice Pudding 126
stock
    chicken 125
    fish 14
Strawberries with Balsamic
    Vinegar 48
Strawberry Fields Salad 146
Strudel Biscuits (Rugelach) 16
Stuffed Artichokes 70
Stuffed Tomatoes 62

Stuffed Vine Leaves 83
sushi
    Roll-your-own Sushi (Temaki
      Sushi) 106
Sweet and Sour Chickpeas 90
Sweet Biscuits (Kichel) 149
Sweet Dumplings (Vareniki) 24
sweet potato
    Rishe's Sweet Potato Pie 175

T
Tabbouleh 81
tahini sauce 84
Tarte aux Fruits 32
tarts
    Fruit Tart 32
    Grenadilla (Passionfruit) Tart 157
Temaki Sushi 106
tiramisu
    Non-dairy Tiramisu 134
tomatoes
    Cooked Salad (Madbucha) 69
    Cucumber, Tomato and Onion
    Salad 89
    Fusilli with Fresh Tomato Sauce 44
    Polenta Gnocchi with a Rich
      Tomato Sauce and Fresh
      Herbs 166
    Stuffed Tomatoes 62
    Tomatoes Stuffed with Rice 43
Tweed Kettle 53
Tyler, Katalin 33–9

V
Vareniki 24
vegetables
    Chicken and Vegetable Soup 36
    Lamb Stew (Chanahi) 8
    Moroccan Couscous with Beef
      and Vegetables 141
    Pickled Vegetables 131
    Ratatouille 139
    Roasted Vegetable Salad 72
    see also particular vegetables
Vietnamese Beef Salad 126
Vietnamese Rice Noodle Soup
    (Pho Ga) 125
Vietnamese Spring Rolls 123
vinaigrette dressing 29
vine leaves
    Stuffed Vine Leaves 83

W
Winter Warmer Chicken 115

Z
Zeesy's Pea Soup 173
Zöldség Leves 36
zucchini
    Etty's Zucchini Kugel 175
    Zucchini Antipasto (Concia) 47

Acknowledgements

We thank each cook for sharing their precious stories and recipes: MIRIAM ATZIL, YAFFA BARAK, JUANITA BEKINSCHTEIN, RAQUELLA BIRNER, PERLA CAVIGLIA, JUNE EDELMUTH, HANNAH ELIJAH, DINA GOLDSCHLAGER, MIRIAM GREENFIELD, RIVKAH GRONER, SHIRLEY HIRSH, NITA JAWARY, BRAM KHAZAM, EVA KEINAN, LUBA KOJIA, DELIA AND LANA RAIZON, SUZANNE RESS, SUSIE ROITMAN, YOKO RYAN, HAZEL SHAPIRO AND KATALIN TYLER.

We are grateful to Kirsten Abbott, for her inspired vision in making our dream come true; Emma Schwarcz, editor at Hardie Grant Books, for bringing everything together with grace and good humour; Sally Moss, for her editing finesse; Marcelle Munro, for assistance with recipes; Trisha Garner for her beautiful design; Meera Freeman, for advice on recipes; Debbie Pack; Alan Goldstone from Tisher Liner & Co. for legal advice; Shareen Joel; and our loving families for being part of this delectable journey. In particular, Hayley thanks Michael, Ruby, Amber, Bronson and Poppy, as well as Romi Pack and Judy Pack; Gaye thanks Philip, Hunter, Charlie, Allegra and Lucas; and Natalie thanks David, Lilly and Coco Weissman, as well as her friend Kate Mizrahi, for lending her wonderful library of cookbooks.

A percentage of profits will be donated to WIZO Golan.

OLOMO

MATZ
MEAL
COARS

NET 375

UNDER STRICT SUPERVISION OF SYDNEY
MANUFACTURED BY A. HALLIS
N.S.W. MATZOS CO.
136-140 COPE ST, WATERLOO
PHONE 698 604

MADE IN AUSTRALIA

NET

CO
M
N

UNDER STRICT SUPERVISION OF
MANUFACTURED BY A. HA
N.S.W. MATZO
136 COPE ST, WATER
PHONE 698 604

MADE IN AUST